Flora and Function

How Plants Shape Our World and Well-being

Juniper Hill

Flora and Function

Table of contents

Chapter 1: The Integral Role of Flora in Our World

The Historical Significance of Plants

The tapestry of human history is intricately woven with the threads of flora, each plant telling its own story of survival, adaptation, and influence. From the earliest whispers of civilization, plants have been more than mere backdrops to human progress; they have been active participants, shaping cultures, economies, and even the very landscapes upon which societies stand. In the fertile crescent of Mesopotamia, wheat and barley were more than crops—they were cornerstones of urbanization, allowing ancient peoples to settle, farm, and ultimately lay the foundations of modern society. These grains were not merely sustenance; they were catalysts for the development of trade, language, and technology.

The significance of plants is not confined to the cradle of civilization. Across the globe, ancient cultures revered flora for their mystical, medicinal, and nutritional properties. The Egyptians, for instance, worshipped the papyrus plant, which was used not only for paper but also for crafting boats and building materials, underscoring its multifaceted importance. Meanwhile, the Native American tribes of North America cultivated maize, beans, and squash—the "Three Sisters"—in a harmonious agricultural trio that provided balanced nutrition and sustainable soil management. These plants were not just food; they were integral to the spiritual and social fabric of their communities.

Plants have also served as silent witnesses to humanity's most profound transformations. The spice trade, fueled by the allure of exotic plants like cinnamon, pepper, and nutmeg, forged new global connections and rivalries during the Age of Exploration. This desire for botanical treasures led to the establishment of trade routes spanning continents and oceans, reshaping political boundaries and cultural exchanges. The pursuit of these spices was a driving force behind the expansion of empires and the birth of modern globalization.

The botanical realm further influenced the course of history through the Industrial Revolution. Cotton, a plant with humble origins, became the linchpin of the textile industry, propelling economic growth and technological innovation. The cultivation and processing of cotton fibers spurred advancements in machinery, transportation, and manufacturing, transforming societies and economies in unprecedented ways. However, this progress was not without its costs, as the demand for cotton also fueled social upheaval and exploitation, particularly in the form of slavery and colonialism.

In the realm of medicine, plants have long been revered as healers and protectors. Ancient texts from China, India, and the Mediterranean reveal a deep understanding of herbal remedies, with plants like willow bark and ginseng providing relief and healing for countless ailments. These botanical medicines laid the groundwork for modern pharmacology, their compounds inspiring the development of synthetic drugs that continue to save millions of lives. The historical significance of medicinal plants is a testament to their enduring legacy as both ancient teachers and modern saviors.

Plants have also played a crucial role in shaping cultural identities and spiritual beliefs. The lotus, revered in both Hinduism and Buddhism, symbolizes purity and enlightenment, transcending its aquatic origins to become a universal emblem of spiritual growth. Similarly, the olive branch, a symbol of peace and victory, has its roots in ancient Greek mythology and continues to carry profound significance in contemporary times. These cultural symbols highlight the deep connection between plants and the human psyche, illustrating how flora can embody ideals and aspirations that transcend generations.

The agricultural revolution, a pivotal moment in human history, was inextricably linked to the domestication and cultivation of plants. The transition from hunter-gatherer societies to settled agricultural communities was marked by the careful selection and breeding of crops, leading to the development of staple foods that could sustain growing populations. This agricultural transformation enabled the rise of civilizations, allowing for the establishment of cities, the division of labor, and the accumulation of surplus resources. Plants, in their varied and versatile forms, were the bedrock upon which these early societies were built.

Beyond their economic and cultural contributions, plants have also served as inspiration for artistic and intellectual endeavors. The beauty and diversity of the botanical world have captivated artists, poets, and scientists alike, inspiring masterpieces and groundbreaking discoveries. The intricate botanical illustrations of the Renaissance, for example, were not only works of art but also valuable scientific documents that advanced the understanding of plant anatomy and classification. Similarly, the study of plant genetics and evolution has provided profound insights into the mechanisms of life itself, influencing fields as diverse as biology, anthropology, and environmental science.

The historical significance of plants is also evident in their role as agents of environmental change. Through the process of photosynthesis, plants have shaped the Earth's atmosphere, influencing climate patterns and sustaining life on a global scale. Forests, in particular, have acted as vital carbon sinks, mitigating the impacts of human-induced climate change and providing essential ecosystem services. The loss of these vital ecosystems due to deforestation and habitat destruction underscores the delicate balance between human progress and environmental stewardship, a theme that resonates throughout history.

In the modern era, the legacy of plants continues to evolve as we face unprecedented challenges and opportunities. The quest for sustainable development and environmental conservation has rekindled interest in the ancient wisdom of plant-based solutions. From renewable resources and green technologies to permaculture and agroforestry, plants offer promising pathways to address some of the most pressing issues of our time. By harnessing the power of plants, we can create resilient systems that honor the past while paving the way for a more sustainable future.

Throughout history, plants have been both humble servants and mighty influencers, their significance etched into the annals of time. As we reflect on their historical contributions, we are reminded of the profound interconnectedness between humanity and the botanical world. The stories of plants are, in essence, the stories of us all, a testament to the enduring bond between nature and humankind.

Plants as the Foundation of Ecosystems

The intricate web of life on Earth owes much of its complexity and resilience to plants, which serve as the cornerstone of ecosystems across the globe. From the towering canopies of rainforests to the sparse vegetation of deserts, plants form the primary producers at the base of the food chain, capturing sunlight and converting it into energy through photosynthesis. This energy not only sustains the plants themselves but also powers the entire ecosystem, supporting a diverse array of organisms from herbivores to apex predators.

The role of plants as foundational elements of ecosystems extends beyond mere energy production. They provide essential habitat and shelter for countless species, creating microenvironments that support a rich tapestry of biodiversity. In forests, the layers of vegetation—from the forest floor to the canopy—offer niches for various animals, insects, and microorganisms. These layers promote a dynamic ecological balance, with each species playing a specific role in maintaining the health and stability of the ecosystem.

Plants also play a crucial role in nutrient cycling, a process integral to the functioning of ecosystems. Through the decomposition of plant material, nutrients such as nitrogen, phosphorus, and potassium are released back into the soil, replenishing the nutrients and fostering new plant growth. This cyclical process ensures the sustainability of ecosystems, allowing them to thrive over time. The root systems of plants further contribute by preventing soil erosion, stabilizing the ground, and maintaining soil structure, which is vital for water retention and aeration.

In aquatic ecosystems, plants such as algae and seagrasses perform similar foundational functions. Algae, for instance, are primary producers in marine environments, forming the base of the food web and supporting a myriad of marine organisms. Seagrasses, on the other hand, provide habitat and breeding grounds for fish and invertebrates, while also stabilizing sediment and improving water quality through nutrient uptake.

Plants are also pivotal in regulating local and global climates. Forests, especially tropical rainforests, act as significant carbon sinks, absorbing carbon dioxide from the atmosphere and mitigating the effects of climate change. Through the process of transpiration, plants release water vapor into the atmosphere, influencing weather patterns and contributing to the formation of clouds and precipitation. This regulation of the water cycle is essential for maintaining the climate stability that supports life on Earth.

The interdependence between plants and other organisms in ecosystems is a testament to the complexity of ecological relationships. Pollinators such as bees, butterflies, and birds rely on plants for nectar and pollen, while plants depend on these animals for reproduction and genetic diversity. This symbiotic relationship highlights the delicate balance of ecosystems, where the decline of one species can have cascading effects on others. activities, however, pose significant threats to the foundational role of plants in ecosystems. Deforestation, habitat destruction, and pollution disrupt the intricate balance of ecosystems, leading to biodiversity loss and ecosystem degradation. The removal of plant cover not only reduces the availability of food and habitat for countless species but also diminishes the ecosystem services that plants provide, such as carbon sequestration and water purification.

Efforts to conserve and restore plant communities are therefore crucial for the health and resilience of ecosystems. Conservation strategies include protecting natural habitats, restoring degraded areas, and promoting sustainable land-use practices. By preserving plant diversity, we can safeguard the ecological functions that support life on Earth and ensure the continued provision of essential ecosystem services.

In agricultural landscapes, the integration of native plants and the practice of agroforestry can enhance ecosystem resilience and productivity. Native plants offer habitat for beneficial insects and birds, contributing to natural pest control and pollination. Agroforestry, which combines trees and shrubs with crops and livestock, promotes biodiversity, soil fertility, and water management, creating sustainable agricultural systems that mimic natural ecosystems.

Urban environments also benefit from the incorporation of plants in the form of green spaces, urban forests, and vertical gardens. These green infrastructures not only improve air and water quality but also provide habitat for urban wildlife and recreational opportunities for people. The presence of plants in cities enhances the quality of life, reduces urban heat islands, and fosters a connection between people and nature.

The foundational role of plants in ecosystems underscores the importance of maintaining plant diversity and abundance across the planet. By understanding and appreciating the vital functions that plants serve, we can make informed decisions that support ecological balance and sustainability. Plants, in their myriad forms and functions, are indispensable to the web of life, offering solutions to some of the most pressing environmental challenges of our time.

As stewards of the planet, it is incumbent upon us to protect and nurture the plant life that sustains ecosystems and, by extension, all life on Earth. Through conservation, restoration, and sustainable practices, we can ensure that plants continue to fulfill their foundational role, supporting the diverse and interconnected tapestry of life that makes our world so vibrant and resilient.

The Interdependence of Plants and Climate

The relationship between plants and climate is a finely tuned symphony, each element influencing the other in an ongoing dance of cause and effect. This interdependence is fundamental to the health and stability of ecosystems worldwide. Plants, through the process of photosynthesis, absorb carbon dioxide from the atmosphere and release oxygen, playing a critical role in regulating atmospheric gases. This process not only supports life on Earth by providing breathable air but also helps to mitigate the effects of climate change by reducing greenhouse gases.

Forests, often referred to as the lungs of the planet, are particularly significant in this regard. They sequester vast amounts of carbon, acting as a buffer against the increasing concentrations of carbon dioxide resulting from human activities. The Amazon rainforest alone, with its dense canopy and rich biodiversity, absorbs millions of tons of carbon each year, helping to stabilize global climate patterns. However, deforestation and land-use changes threaten these vital functions, releasing stored carbon back into the atmosphere and contributing to global warming.

The climate also profoundly influences plant growth and distribution. Temperature, sunlight, and rainfall are key factors that determine which plant species can thrive in a given area. As climate patterns shift due to global warming, plants are forced to adapt, migrate, or face potential extinction. Alpine plants, for instance, are pushed to higher altitudes as temperatures rise, while desert plants must cope with changes in precipitation and increased aridity. These shifts not only affect individual species but also the structure and composition of entire ecosystems, leading to cascading effects on biodiversity and ecosystem services.

Plants are not mere spectators in the face of climate change; they are active participants in shaping their environment. Through processes such as evapotranspiration, plants release water vapor into the atmosphere, influencing local climates and contributing to the formation of clouds and precipitation. This feedback loop is essential for maintaining the water cycle, which in turn supports plant growth and sustains life in various ecosystems. The loss of vegetation cover, particularly in arid and semi-arid regions, can disrupt this cycle, leading to desertification and further exacerbating climate impacts.

In coastal regions, mangroves and salt marshes act as natural buffers against the impacts of climate change. These unique plant communities protect shorelines from erosion, storm surges, and rising sea levels. By stabilizing sediments and reducing wave energy, they help to safeguard coastal ecosystems and human settlements. Furthermore, these habitats are highly efficient carbon sinks, sequestering carbon at rates comparable to or even exceeding those of terrestrial forests. The conservation and restoration of these blue carbon ecosystems are crucial for enhancing climate resilience and supporting biodiversity.

The interplay between plants and climate is also evident in agricultural systems. Farmers have long relied on their understanding of climatic conditions to optimize crop yields and sustain food production. However, climate change poses significant challenges to agriculture, with shifting weather patterns and increased incidence of extreme events such as droughts and floods. These changes necessitate adaptive strategies, including the development of climate-resilient crops, improved irrigation techniques, and sustainable farming practices that enhance soil health and reduce emissions.

Urban environments present unique opportunities and challenges in the context of plants and climate. Green spaces, urban forests, and green roofs can mitigate the urban heat island effect, improve air quality, and enhance the overall livability of cities. By integrating plants into urban planning and design, cities can become more resilient to climate impacts while providing essential ecosystem services. The use of native and drought-tolerant species, for instance, can reduce water usage and maintenance costs, contributing to sustainable urban development.

The interdependence of plants and climate is a reminder of the delicate balance that sustains life on Earth. As we face the realities of climate change, it is imperative to recognize the vital role that plants play in maintaining this balance. Conservation efforts, reforestation initiatives, and sustainable land management practices are essential for preserving the ecological functions that plants provide. By fostering a harmonious relationship between plants and climate, we can safeguard the health of our planet and ensure a sustainable future for generations to come.

Understanding this intricate relationship also offers valuable insights for climate adaptation and mitigation strategies. By leveraging the natural abilities of plants to sequester carbon, regulate water cycles, and protect ecosystems, we can develop innovative solutions to combat climate change. Restoration of degraded landscapes, protection of existing forests, and the expansion of green infrastructure are just a few examples of how plants can be harnessed to enhance climate resilience.

In conclusion, the interdependence of plants and climate is a cornerstone of ecological stability and sustainability. Recognizing and nurturing this relationship is essential for addressing the challenges of climate change and preserving the natural world upon which we all depend. Through informed actions and collaborative efforts, we can create a future where plants and climate exist in harmony, supporting the diverse web of life that makes our planet unique.

Key Concepts in Plant Ecology

Plant ecology delves into the intricate relationships between plants and their environment, exploring how they interact with one another and the myriad of organisms that share their habitat. At its core, plant ecology seeks to understand the distribution and abundance of plant species, the dynamics of plant communities, and the processes that drive these patterns. This field is a cornerstone of ecological study, providing insights that guide conservation efforts, inform land management, and enhance our understanding of the biosphere.

One of the foundational concepts in plant ecology is the notion of the ecological niche, which refers to the role a plant species plays within its ecosystem. This includes its requirements for resources such as light, water, and nutrients, as well as its interactions with other organisms. The concept of the niche helps explain why certain plants thrive in specific environments while others do not. For instance, cacti have evolved to occupy niches in arid deserts, where they efficiently store water and reduce transpiration, whereas ferns find their niche in moist, shaded forests.

The study of plant communities, or the assemblages of different plant species living together, is another key aspect of plant ecology. These communities are shaped by a combination of biotic and abiotic factors, including competition, herbivory, soil composition, temperature, and precipitation. Understanding the composition and structure of plant communities sheds light on the complex interactions that sustain ecosystems. In a tropical rainforest, for example, the diversity of plant species is so vast that it creates a multi-layered canopy, each layer supporting different organisms and ecological processes.

Succession is a dynamic concept in plant ecology that describes the gradual process by which plant communities change over time following a disturbance, such as a fire, flood, or human activity. Primary succession occurs in previously uninhabited areas, like volcanic islands or glacial retreats, where pioneer species colonize the bare substrate and pave the way for more complex communities. Secondary succession, on the other hand, takes place in areas where a disturbance has altered existing communities but left the soil intact. Over time, these successional stages lead to a climax community, a stable and mature ecosystem that persists until the next disturbance.

The concept of biodiversity is central to plant ecology, emphasizing the variety of life forms within an ecosystem. Biodiversity is not just about the number of species, but also the genetic diversity within those species and the diversity of ecosystems themselves. High biodiversity is often associated with greater resilience, as diverse plant communities can better withstand environmental changes and disturbances. The loss of biodiversity, whether through habitat destruction, invasive species, or climate change, poses significant threats to ecosystem stability and function.

Plant ecology also examines the interactions between plants and other organisms, including mutualism, predation, and competition. Mutualistic relationships, such as those between flowering plants and their pollinators or mycorrhizal fungi and plant roots, are vital for the survival and reproduction of many plant species. Herbivory, where animals feed on plants, is a form of predation that exerts selective pressure on plants, leading to the evolution of defensive traits like thorns, toxins, and tough leaves. Competition among plants for resources like light, water, and nutrients influences their growth patterns and spatial distribution, shaping the structure of plant communities.

The flow of energy and nutrients through ecosystems is another critical area of study in plant ecology. Plants, as primary producers, capture solar energy through photosynthesis and convert it into biomass, which then supports herbivores, carnivores, and decomposers. The cycling of nutrients such as carbon, nitrogen, and phosphorus is essential for maintaining ecosystem productivity and health. Decomposers, including bacteria and fungi, play a key role in breaking down organic matter and returning nutrients to the soil, where they become available for plant uptake once again. activities have profound impacts on plant ecology, altering ecosystems and the processes that sustain them. Deforestation, urbanization, pollution, and climate change disrupt plant communities and their ecological roles, leading to habitat loss, species extinctions, and reduced ecosystem services. Understanding plant ecology is therefore crucial for developing strategies to mitigate these impacts and promote environmental sustainability. This includes restoring degraded ecosystems, conserving biodiversity, and implementing sustainable land-use practices that balance human needs with ecological integrity.

Ecologists often use models and experiments to study plant ecology, seeking to unravel the complex interactions and processes that govern ecosystems. Field studies, where researchers observe and measure plants in their natural habitats, provide valuable data on species distribution, population dynamics, and community structure. Controlled experiments, conducted in laboratories or field plots, allow scientists to test hypotheses about specific ecological processes, such as the effects of competition or nutrient availability on plant growth.

The study of plant ecology is not only about understanding the natural world but also about applying this knowledge to address real-world challenges. As human populations grow and environmental pressures intensify, the insights gained from plant ecology become increasingly important for guiding conservation efforts, informing policy decisions, and fostering a more sustainable relationship with the planet. By appreciating the complexity and interconnectedness of plant life, we can better protect the ecosystems that support us all.

Plant ecology is a vibrant and evolving field that continues to uncover the mysteries of the natural world. Its key concepts provide a framework for understanding the diversity and dynamics of plant life, highlighting the intricate relationships that sustain ecosystems. Through research and application, plant ecologists contribute to a deeper appreciation of the environment and the development of solutions to the ecological challenges we face. As we continue to explore and learn, the knowledge gained from plant ecology will play a vital role in shaping a sustainable future for both people and nature.

Understanding Biodiversity and Its Importance

Biodiversity, a term encompassing the vast variety of life on Earth, is a concept as rich and complex as the ecosystems it describes. It includes the diversity of species, genetic variations within those species, and the myriad of ecosystems they form. This diversity is not merely an academic curiosity; it is the bedrock of ecosystem health and resilience. Understanding biodiversity and its importance reveals the intricate tapestry of life and highlights the essential roles that different life forms play in maintaining ecological balance.

The richness of biodiversity is evident in the staggering number of plant and animal species that inhabit the planet. From the microscopic phytoplankton in the oceans to the towering redwoods of California, each species contributes uniquely to its environment. This diversity ensures that ecosystems are robust and can withstand and adapt to changes, whether they arise from natural events or human activities. The loss of any single species can have unforeseen consequences, potentially disrupting food webs and ecosystem services on which countless other organisms, including humans, rely.

Genetic diversity within species is another crucial aspect of biodiversity. This genetic variability allows populations to adapt to changing environmental conditions, diseases, and other challenges. It is the raw material for evolution, enabling species to survive and thrive over generations. A population with low genetic diversity is more vulnerable to extinction, as it may lack the necessary traits to cope with environmental stresses. The preservation of genetic diversity is thus vital for the continued survival and adaptability of all species.

Biodiversity also manifests in the form of ecosystems, which are communities of living organisms interacting with their physical environment. These ecosystems, ranging from rainforests and coral reefs to grasslands and wetlands, provide essential services that support life on Earth. They regulate climate, purify air and water, pollinate crops, and decompose organic matter. The intricate interactions within these ecosystems ensure the flow of energy and nutrients, maintaining the balance that sustains life. The degradation of any ecosystem can lead to the loss of these vital services, with profound implications for both nature and humanity.

The importance of biodiversity extends beyond ecological functions; it holds cultural, economic, and intrinsic value. Many cultures around the world have deep spiritual and traditional connections to the natural world, viewing biodiversity as integral to their identity and heritage. Economically, biodiversity underpins industries such as agriculture, pharmaceuticals, and tourism, providing raw materials and inspiration for countless products and services. The genetic resources found in nature are invaluable for developing new crops, medicines, and technologies. Furthermore, biodiversity has intrinsic value, deserving of protection regardless of its utility to humans. Every species has an inherent right to exist, reflecting the wonder and beauty of the natural world.

The current loss of biodiversity, driven by habitat destruction, climate change, pollution, and overexploitation, is a pressing global challenge. This biodiversity crisis threatens the stability and resilience of ecosystems, with cascading effects on all life forms, including humans. The loss of pollinators, for example, can jeopardize food security by reducing crop yields, while the decline of coral reefs diminishes marine biodiversity and the livelihoods of communities dependent on them. The urgency to address biodiversity loss is underscored by its far-reaching impacts on ecosystems, economies, and cultures worldwide.

Conservation efforts play a pivotal role in safeguarding biodiversity. Protected areas, such as national parks and wildlife reserves, are essential for preserving habitats and species. These areas provide refuges where ecosystems can function without the pressures of human activities. Conservation biology, a scientific discipline dedicated to understanding and mitigating biodiversity loss, employs a variety of strategies to protect species and their habitats.

These include habitat restoration, the reintroduction of endangered species, and the establishment of wildlife corridors that connect fragmented habitats.

Sustainable practices in agriculture, forestry, and fisheries are crucial for maintaining biodiversity. By adopting methods that minimize environmental impacts, such as organic farming, agroforestry, and sustainable fishing, we can reduce the pressures on ecosystems and promote biodiversity. Integrated land-use planning, which considers the needs of both humans and nature, can create landscapes that support biodiversity while meeting human demands for resources.

The role of individuals and communities in promoting biodiversity cannot be overstated. Local and indigenous communities often possess invaluable traditional knowledge about biodiversity and sustainable resource management. By involving these communities in conservation efforts and respecting their rights and wisdom, we can enhance the effectiveness of biodiversity protection. Individuals, too, can contribute by making environmentally conscious choices, such as reducing waste, supporting sustainable products, and participating in citizen science initiatives that monitor and protect biodiversity.

Education and awareness are powerful tools for fostering an appreciation of biodiversity and its importance. By learning about the diverse species and ecosystems that make up our world, people can develop a sense of stewardship and responsibility for protecting nature. Educational programs, from school curricula to public outreach campaigns, can inspire a new generation of environmental advocates and empower individuals to take action for biodiversity conservation.

The interconnectedness of all life forms is a fundamental principle of biodiversity. Understanding this interconnectedness helps us appreciate the complexity and beauty of the natural world and underscores our responsibility to protect it. Biodiversity is not merely a backdrop to human existence; it is the foundation upon which our lives depend. By valuing and conserving biodiversity, we can ensure a healthy, vibrant planet for current and future generations.

Biodiversity, in all its forms, is a testament to the resilience and adaptability of life on Earth. As we deepen our understanding of its significance, we find not only the keys to ecological health but also a source of inspiration and wonder. The protection and preservation of biodiversity are not merely scientific or economic endeavors; they are moral imperatives that reflect our respect for the natural world and our commitment to living in harmony with it. Through concerted efforts and a shared vision, we can overcome the challenges facing biodiversity and secure a sustainable future for all life on this planet.

Chapter 2: How Plants Influence Our Environment

The Role of Photosynthesis in Earth's Atmosphere

Photosynthesis stands as one of the most transformative processes on Earth, fundamentally altering the composition of our planet's atmosphere and shaping the environment in which life thrives. This remarkable biochemical process enables plants, algae, and some bacteria to convert sunlight into chemical energy, using water and carbon dioxide to produce glucose and oxygen. The implications of photosynthesis extend far beyond the organisms that perform it, as it plays a critical role in sustaining life and maintaining atmospheric balance.

The origins of photosynthesis trace back over three billion years, when early photosynthetic organisms began harnessing sunlight to produce energy. This evolutionary leap not only provided these organisms with a competitive advantage but also initiated a profound transformation of Earth's atmosphere. Before the advent of photosynthesis, the atmosphere was dominated by gases such as methane, ammonia, and carbon dioxide, with little to no oxygen. The gradual accumulation of oxygen produced by photosynthesis led to the Great Oxidation Event, a pivotal moment in Earth's history that paved the way for aerobic life forms and more complex ecosystems.

Oxygen, a byproduct of photosynthesis, is essential for the survival of most life forms on Earth. It fuels cellular respiration, a process that allows organisms to convert nutrients into energy. The abundance of oxygen in the atmosphere, maintained by continuous photosynthetic activity, supports diverse life forms, from microscopic bacteria to large mammals. The delicate balance of oxygen production and consumption is crucial for maintaining this life-supporting environment, highlighting the indispensable role of photosynthesis in sustaining life.

Beyond oxygen production, photosynthesis plays a vital role in the carbon cycle, a series of processes that regulate the flow of carbon between the atmosphere, oceans, and land. Through photosynthesis, plants absorb carbon dioxide from the atmosphere, incorporating it into organic molecules that fuel their growth. This process not only reduces atmospheric carbon dioxide levels but also stores carbon in plant biomass, soils, and other organic matter. In turn, this storage helps mitigate the effects of climate change by sequestering carbon that would otherwise contribute to the greenhouse effect.

Forests, particularly tropical rainforests, are often referred to as the planet's lungs due to their significant photosynthetic activity. These ecosystems absorb vast amounts of carbon dioxide, acting as critical carbon sinks that help stabilize global climate patterns. However, deforestation and land-use changes threaten these vital functions, releasing stored carbon back into the atmosphere and exacerbating climate change. The preservation and restoration of forests are therefore essential for maintaining the ecological balance and mitigating global warming.

Photosynthesis also influences the water cycle, another crucial component of Earth's climate system. During photosynthesis, plants release water vapor into the atmosphere through tiny openings in their leaves called stomata. This process, known as transpiration, contributes to cloud formation and precipitation, helping to regulate local and global weather patterns. The presence of vegetation, particularly in large forested areas, plays a critical role in maintaining regional climates and ensuring the availability of freshwater resources.

The impact of photosynthesis extends to aquatic environments as well. Phytoplankton, microscopic photosynthetic organisms found in oceans and freshwater bodies, are responsible for about half of the global photosynthetic activity. These tiny organisms form the base of the marine food web, supporting a vast array of aquatic life, from small fish to large marine mammals. The oxygen and organic matter produced by phytoplankton are essential for the health and productivity of marine ecosystems. The balance of phytoplankton populations is closely linked to nutrient availability and water temperature, making them sensitive indicators of environmental change. activities, particularly the burning of fossil fuels and deforestation, have significant impacts on the processes and balance maintained by photosynthesis. The increased concentration of carbon dioxide in the atmosphere due to these activities enhances the greenhouse effect, leading to global warming and climate change. While higher carbon dioxide levels can stimulate photosynthetic activity in some plants, the overall effects on ecosystems are complex and often detrimental. Changes in temperature and precipitation patterns can alter plant growth and distribution, affecting biodiversity and ecosystem services.

Efforts to harness and enhance the benefits of photosynthesis are at the forefront of strategies to address climate change and promote sustainability. Reforestation and afforestation initiatives aim to increase the number of trees and plants, boosting photosynthetic activity and carbon sequestration. In agriculture, practices such as agroforestry and cover cropping integrate trees and plants into farming systems, enhancing soil health and reducing greenhouse gas emissions. Advances in biotechnology also hold promise for improving photosynthetic efficiency in crops, potentially increasing yields and reducing the need for agricultural land expansion.

Understanding the role of photosynthesis in Earth's atmosphere is crucial for appreciating the interconnectedness of life and the environment. This knowledge underscores the importance of preserving natural ecosystems and promoting sustainable practices that support photosynthetic processes. By fostering a deeper awareness of the vital functions photosynthesis performs, we can make informed decisions that contribute to the health and resilience of our planet.

The story of photosynthesis is one of transformation and balance, a testament to the power of life to shape its environment. As we continue to explore and understand this process, we recognize its central role in supporting life on Earth and the responsibility we have to protect and sustain it. Through collective action and a commitment to stewardship, we can ensure that photosynthesis continues to perform its life-sustaining functions, benefiting not only the present generation but also those to come.

Plants in Water Cycle Regulation

Water, the lifeblood of Earth, circulates through a complex system known as the water cycle, a continuous movement that sustains ecosystems and supports life. Plants play a crucial role in regulating this cycle, influencing everything from local weather patterns to global climate. Their interactions with water are multifaceted, involving processes such as absorption, transpiration, and precipitation, each contributing to the delicate balance that maintains ecological harmony.

At the heart of this interaction is the process of transpiration, where plants absorb water from the soil through their roots and release it as water vapor through small pores in their leaves called stomata. This release of water vapor into the atmosphere is a vital component of the water cycle, contributing to the formation of clouds and precipitation. Transpiration not only helps maintain atmospheric moisture levels but also cools the plant, facilitating nutrient transport and photosynthesis.

Forests, particularly tropical rainforests, are major players in the global water cycle. These ecosystems transpire vast amounts of water, creating a humid environment that promotes regular rainfall. The Amazon rainforest, for instance, is responsible for generating a significant portion of its own rainfall through a process known as "rain recycling." This self-sustaining system helps regulate the regional climate and influences weather patterns far beyond its borders. The loss of forest cover through deforestation disrupts this cycle, leading to reduced rainfall and altered climate conditions.

In addition to forests, wetlands such as marshes, swamps, and bogs are vital in water cycle regulation. These ecosystems act as natural water storage and filtration systems, absorbing excess water during floods and slowly releasing it during dry periods. Wetlands help maintain the water table, recharge groundwater supplies, and filter pollutants from surface water, ensuring clean and reliable water sources. The destruction of wetlands for agriculture and urban development diminishes these essential services, increasing the risk of flooding and water scarcity.

Plants also play a role in soil moisture regulation, a critical factor in the water cycle. Vegetation cover helps prevent soil erosion and maintains soil structure, allowing for efficient water infiltration and retention. This process reduces surface runoff and promotes groundwater recharge, enhancing the availability of freshwater resources. In agricultural landscapes, practices such as cover cropping and agroforestry integrate plants into farming systems, improving soil health and water management.

The interactions between plants and the water cycle extend to urban environments as well. Trees and green spaces in cities mitigate the urban heat island effect, reduce stormwater runoff, and improve air quality. Urban forests and green roofs capture rainwater, reducing the burden on drainage systems and minimizing the risk of flooding. By incorporating vegetation into urban planning, cities can enhance their resilience to climate impacts and create healthier living environments. activities that alter the natural landscape also affect the role of plants in the water cycle. Deforestation, land conversion, and the drainage of wetlands disrupt the balance of water movements, leading to changes in precipitation patterns, increased frequency of extreme weather events, and reduced water quality. These impacts underscore the importance of conserving natural ecosystems and implementing sustainable land-use practices that support the water cycle's intricate processes.

Efforts to restore and enhance the role of plants in water cycle regulation are gaining momentum worldwide. Reforestation and afforestation projects aim to restore degraded landscapes, increase canopy cover, and improve water management. In agricultural settings, the adoption of sustainable practices such as precision irrigation, organic farming, and permaculture can enhance water use efficiency and support healthy ecosystems. Protecting and restoring wetlands is also crucial for maintaining their water regulation functions and preserving biodiversity.

Education and awareness are essential for fostering an understanding of the connections between plants and the water cycle. By learning about the ecological functions of plants and their role in water regulation, individuals and communities can make informed decisions about resource management and conservation. Educational programs, citizen science initiatives, and community engagement projects can inspire people to take action for water sustainability and ecosystem protection.

The intricate ties between plants and the water cycle illustrate the interconnectedness of life and the environment. Recognizing and nurturing these connections is vital for ensuring the sustainability of our planet's resources. By appreciating the role of plants in water regulation, we can develop strategies that promote ecological balance, support biodiversity, and enhance resilience to environmental change.

In conclusion, plants are indispensable in maintaining the water cycle, a cornerstone of ecological stability and human well-being. Their ability to influence water movements and contribute to climate regulation highlights their essential role in sustaining life on Earth. Through conservation efforts, sustainable practices, and a commitment to environmental stewardship, we can protect and enhance the functions that plants perform in the water cycle, securing a healthy and vibrant future for generations to come.

Soil Formation and Nutrient Cycling

The formation of soil and the cycling of nutrients are fundamental processes that underpin terrestrial ecosystems, providing the foundation for plant growth and sustaining complex food webs. Understanding these processes offers insight into the dynamic interactions between the Earth's surface and the living organisms that inhabit it. Soil is not merely inert material; it is a living system teeming with life, from microorganisms to larger fauna, each playing a crucial role in nutrient cycling and soil health.

Soil formation, or pedogenesis, is a slow and intricate process that transforms raw geological material into fertile ground capable of supporting life. It begins with the weathering of parent rock, a process driven by physical, chemical, and biological factors. Physical weathering breaks down rocks into smaller particles through the action of wind, water, temperature fluctuations, and biological activity. Chemical weathering involves the alteration of minerals within rocks, often accelerated by water and the presence of organic acids produced by plants and microbes. Biological weathering, on the other hand, results from the actions of living organisms, such as plant roots that penetrate rock crevices or lichens that secrete acids to break down rock surfaces.

The resulting material, combined with organic matter from decaying plants and animals, forms the initial layers of soil. Over time, these layers develop into distinct horizons, each with unique physical and chemical properties. The organic-rich topsoil, or the O horizon, is where most biological activity occurs, teeming with microorganisms, insects, and plant roots. Beneath this lies the A horizon, a layer of mineral soil mixed with organic matter, followed by the B horizon, which accumulates leached minerals and nutrients. The deeper C horizon consists of partially weathered parent material, providing a reservoir of minerals that can be gradually integrated into the upper soil layers.

Nutrient cycling within soil is a vital ecological process that ensures the continuous availability of essential elements for plant growth. This cycle involves the decomposition of organic matter, the transformation of nutrients into forms accessible to plants, and the eventual return of these nutrients to the soil. Decomposers, including bacteria, fungi, and detritivores, play a pivotal role in breaking down organic material and releasing nutrients such as nitrogen, phosphorus, and potassium. These nutrients are then assimilated by plants, which use them to build tissues and carry out metabolic processes.

Nitrogen, an essential component of amino acids and nucleic acids, undergoes a complex cycle involving various forms and processes. Nitrogen fixation, carried out by certain bacteria and archaea, converts atmospheric nitrogen into ammonia, a form usable by plants. This process can occur symbiotically, with bacteria living in root nodules of legumes, or nonsymbiotically, with free-living bacteria in the soil. Ammonia is further converted into nitrates through nitrification, a process facilitated by nitrifying bacteria. Plants absorb these nitrates, incorporating them into organic compounds. The nitrogen cycle is completed when decomposers break down organic matter, returning nitrogen to the soil as ammonia, or when denitrifying bacteria convert nitrates back into nitrogen gas, releasing it into the atmosphere.

Phosphorus, another critical nutrient, is primarily derived from the weathering of phosphate-containing rocks.

Unlike nitrogen, phosphorus does not have a gaseous phase and moves through the ecosystem in a more localized cycle. Plants absorb phosphorus in the form of phosphate ions, which are then incorporated into vital molecules such as ATP, nucleic acids, and phospholipids. The return of phosphorus to the soil occurs through the decomposition of organic matter and the mineralization of phosphates by soil microbes.

Soil organisms, from microscopic bacteria to earthworms, are integral to nutrient cycling and soil health. These organisms contribute to the breakdown of organic material, improve soil structure, and facilitate the movement of air and water through the soil. Earthworms, for example, are known as ecosystem engineers due to their ability to enhance soil aeration and drainage, increase nutrient availability, and promote microbial activity. The presence and diversity of soil organisms are indicators of soil health and fertility, with healthy soils supporting a rich and varied community of life. activities, such as agriculture, deforestation, and urbanization, can significantly impact soil formation and nutrient cycling. Intensive farming practices, including monoculture and excessive use of chemical fertilizers, deplete soil nutrients, reduce organic matter, and diminish soil biodiversity. Soil erosion, a consequence of deforestation and poor land management, removes the nutrient-rich topsoil, leading to reduced soil fertility and increased vulnerability to degradation. Urbanization, with its impervious surfaces and altered landscapes, disrupts natural soil processes and reduces the availability of land for agriculture and habitat.

Sustainable land management practices are essential for preserving soil health and ensuring the continued cycling of nutrients. Techniques such as crop rotation, cover cropping, and conservation tillage help maintain soil fertility, reduce erosion, and support biodiversity. Organic farming, which emphasizes the use of natural fertilizers and compost, enhances soil structure and promotes the activity of beneficial soil organisms. Reforestation and afforestation efforts can restore degraded lands, improve soil quality, and support the natural processes of soil formation and nutrient cycling.

Education and awareness about the importance of soil health and nutrient cycling are crucial for fostering a sustainable relationship with the land. By understanding the intricate processes that sustain soil ecosystems, individuals and communities can make informed decisions about land use and resource management. Educational initiatives, community gardens, and citizen science projects can engage people in soil conservation efforts, promoting stewardship and resilience in the face of environmental challenges.

The dynamic processes of soil formation and nutrient cycling are foundational to the health and productivity of ecosystems. Recognizing the vital role that soils play in supporting life encourages a deeper appreciation for the interconnectedness of natural systems and the need to protect and enhance these essential resources. Through sustainable practices and a commitment to conservation, we can ensure that soils continue to provide the nutrients and support necessary for a thriving and resilient planet.

Plant Adaptations to Environmental Changes

Plants, the silent sentinels of nature, have developed an extraordinary arsenal of adaptations that enable them to survive and thrive in diverse environments. These adaptations, honed through millions of years of evolution, allow plants to respond to the myriad challenges posed by their surroundings, from extreme temperatures and limited water availability to varying light conditions and nutrient scarcity. Understanding these adaptations illuminates the resilience and ingenuity of plant life, offering insights into how these organisms navigate the complexities of their habitats.

In arid environments, where water is a precious commodity, plants have evolved remarkable strategies to conserve moisture and endure prolonged periods of drought. Succulents, such as cacti and aloes, store water in their fleshy tissues, allowing them to survive long stretches without rainfall. Their thick, waxy cuticles reduce water loss through evaporation, while their spines provide shade and protect against herbivores. Some desert plants exhibit a phenomenon known as CAM (Crassulacean Acid Metabolism) photosynthesis, where they open their stomata at night to minimize water loss while still acquiring carbon dioxide for photosynthesis. This nocturnal activity allows them to continue metabolic processes without exposing themselves to the harsh daytime heat.

In contrast, plants in waterlogged environments, such as marshes and swamps, face the challenge of obtaining sufficient oxygen for root respiration. To overcome this, many wetland plants have developed aerenchyma, specialized tissue with air-filled channels that facilitate the transport of oxygen from the leaves to the roots. This adaptation enables plants like rice and mangroves to thrive in saturated soils, where oxygen is limited. Some aquatic plants, such as water lilies, have leaves with a large surface area and air spaces that help them float, maximizing their exposure to sunlight for photosynthesis.

Extreme temperatures, whether scorching heat or biting cold, present another set of challenges for plants. In cold climates, plants have evolved strategies to prevent freezing damage and ensure survival through harsh winters. Deciduous trees, for example, shed their leaves to conserve energy and reduce water loss during the cold months. Many perennials retreat underground, storing nutrients in bulbs or tubers until conditions become favorable for growth. In alpine regions, plants often grow close to the ground, forming cushion-like structures that reduce exposure to cold winds and trap heat.

Conversely, in hot climates, plants must contend with intense sunlight and high temperatures that can damage tissues and disrupt photosynthesis. Some plants have developed reflective leaf surfaces or dense hair coverings that deflect sunlight and reduce heat absorption. Others, like the creosote bush, have small, waxy leaves that minimize water loss and withstand the desert sun. Additionally, many plants exhibit physiological adaptations, such as heat-shock proteins, that protect cellular structures from temperature-induced stress.

Light availability is a critical factor influencing plant growth and development. In dense forests, where sunlight is a limited resource, plants have evolved various strategies to capture light. Shade-tolerant species, such as ferns and mosses, can photosynthesize efficiently under low-light conditions, while others, like lianas and epiphytes, climb or attach themselves to taller trees to reach the canopy. In contrast, plants in open, sun-drenched environments often possess adaptations to prevent damage from intense light, such as protective pigments that shield chlorophyll from UV radiation.

Nutrient availability, or lack thereof, is another environmental factor that plants must navigate. In nutrient-poor soils, some plants have formed mutualistic relationships with fungi, known as mycorrhizae, which enhance nutrient uptake. These fungi extend the root system's reach, allowing plants to access nutrients that would otherwise be unavailable. Other plants, such as legumes, host nitrogen-fixing bacteria within their root nodules, converting atmospheric nitrogen into a form they can use. In environments where nutrients are scarce, some plants, like the carnivorous pitcher plant, have developed unique strategies to supplement their diet by capturing and digesting insects.

Beyond these specific adaptations, plants exhibit remarkable plasticity, the ability to modify their growth and development in response to environmental cues. This plasticity allows plants to optimize resource use and maximize survival in changing conditions. For example, plants may alter their root-to-shoot ratio based on water availability, with more resources allocated to root growth in dry conditions to enhance water uptake. Similarly, plants may adjust leaf size, shape, and orientation to optimize light capture and reduce water loss.

The resilience and adaptability of plants are not only a testament to their evolutionary success but also hold valuable lessons for addressing modern environmental challenges. As climate change alters temperature and precipitation patterns, understanding plant adaptations can inform conservation efforts and the development of resilient agricultural systems. By selecting or breeding crop varieties with traits suited to changing climates, we can enhance food security and reduce the environmental impact of agriculture.

In urban environments, where plants face unique challenges such as pollution, limited space, and altered microclimates, selecting species with specific adaptations can enhance green infrastructure and improve urban resilience. Green roofs, vertical gardens, and urban forests can benefit from plants that tolerate heat, drought, and poor soil conditions, contributing to cooler cities and improved air quality.

Education and public awareness play a crucial role in fostering appreciation for the adaptability and resilience of plants. By understanding the diverse strategies plants use to navigate their environments, individuals and communities can develop a deeper connection to the natural world and support conservation and sustainable practices. Educational initiatives, botanic gardens, and citizen science projects can engage people in exploring plant diversity and the importance of preserving habitats that support these remarkable organisms.

The myriad adaptations exhibited by plants highlight the intricate interplay between organisms and their environments. These adaptations not only ensure the survival of individual species but also contribute to the stability and resilience of ecosystems. By embracing the lessons plants offer, we can enhance our ability to coexist with the natural world and address the environmental challenges of the future. The ingenuity of plant adaptations serves as a reminder of the resilience inherent in nature and the potential for innovation and adaptation in the face of change.

The Impact of Urban Green Spaces

Urban green spaces, those pockets of nature nestled within the concrete jungles of cities, are more than just aesthetic additions to urban landscapes. They are vital components of urban ecosystems, offering a myriad of benefits that enhance the quality of life for city dwellers while promoting environmental sustainability. These spaces, which include parks, gardens, green roofs, and urban forests, serve as sanctuaries of biodiversity, mitigating the effects of urbanization and fostering a connection between people and nature.

In the hustle and bustle of urban life, green spaces provide essential refuge and recreation, offering residents a chance to unwind and rejuvenate. The presence of trees, grass, and flowers has a calming effect, reducing stress and improving mental health. Research has shown that access to green spaces is associated with lower levels of anxiety and depression, highlighting the therapeutic value of nature in urban settings. The opportunity to exercise, socialize, or simply relax in a park contributes to a healthier lifestyle, fostering a sense of community and well-being.

Beyond their impact on human health, urban green spaces play a crucial role in enhancing air quality. Trees and plants act as natural air filters, absorbing pollutants such as carbon dioxide, sulfur dioxide, and particulate matter. Through the process of photosynthesis, they release oxygen, improving the air we breathe. The cooling effect of trees, known as evapotranspiration, further enhances air quality by reducing the urban heat island effect. This phenomenon, caused by the concentration of heat-absorbing materials like asphalt and concrete, leads to higher temperatures in cities compared to surrounding rural areas. Green spaces help moderate these temperature extremes, making cities more comfortable and reducing energy consumption for cooling purposes.

The ecological benefits of urban green spaces extend to water management as well. Vegetation helps regulate the water cycle by absorbing rainwater, reducing surface runoff, and replenishing groundwater supplies. Green roofs, in particular, are effective at capturing and retaining stormwater, alleviating pressure on urban drainage systems and reducing the risk of flooding. By filtering pollutants from rainwater, green spaces also improve water quality, contributing to healthier urban waterways.

Urban green spaces serve as havens for biodiversity, providing habitat and resources for a wide range of plant and animal species. Insects, birds, and small mammals find refuge in these areas, supporting ecological interactions and maintaining ecosystem health. The presence of diverse flora and fauna in cities enhances the resilience of urban ecosystems, enabling them to withstand environmental pressures and adapt to changing conditions. Efforts to incorporate native plant species into urban landscapes further support local biodiversity, promoting ecological balance and preserving regional heritage.

Community gardens, a specific type of urban green space, offer unique opportunities for social interaction and environmental education. These gardens empower residents to grow their own food, fostering a sense of self-sufficiency and connection to the land. They also serve as platforms for learning, where people of all ages can acquire knowledge about sustainable agriculture, biodiversity, and nutrition. Community gardens promote cultural exchange and inclusivity, bringing together people from diverse backgrounds to share experiences and work towards common goals.

The integration of green spaces into urban planning is essential for creating sustainable cities that prioritize the well-being of their inhabitants. Strategic placement and design of these spaces can maximize their benefits, ensuring accessibility for all residents and enhancing connectivity within the urban fabric. Incorporating green corridors, which link parks and natural areas, facilitates movement for both people and wildlife, promoting ecological continuity and recreation opportunities.

Challenges in maintaining and expanding urban green spaces are numerous, particularly in densely populated areas where land is scarce and expensive. Balancing development needs with environmental preservation requires innovative approaches and collaboration among stakeholders, including city planners, policymakers, and community members. Public participation in the planning and management of green spaces is vital for ensuring that these areas meet the needs and preferences of the communities they serve.

Technological advancements and creative design solutions are paving the way for more effective and sustainable urban green spaces. Green infrastructure, such as living walls and vertical gardens, transforms otherwise unused surfaces into vibrant ecosystems, contributing to urban greening efforts without requiring additional land. Smart technologies, including sensors and data analytics, enable efficient monitoring and maintenance of green spaces, optimizing resource use and enhancing their performance.

The economic benefits of urban green spaces should not be overlooked. These areas can increase property values, attract investment, and stimulate local economies by providing venues for events and tourism. The cost savings associated with green spaces, such as reduced healthcare expenses and energy consumption, further highlight their value as critical urban assets. By recognizing the multifaceted contributions of green spaces, cities can leverage them as tools for economic development and resilience.

Education and awareness initiatives are crucial for fostering a culture of stewardship and appreciation for urban green spaces. Schools, community organizations, and local governments can play a pivotal role in promoting environmental literacy and encouraging active engagement with green spaces. Programs that involve citizens in planting, maintaining, and enjoying these areas cultivate a sense of ownership and responsibility, ensuring the long-term success of urban greening efforts.

In an era of rapid urbanization and environmental change, the significance of urban green spaces cannot be overstated. They are essential components of sustainable cities, providing ecological, social, and economic benefits that enhance the quality of life for all residents. By prioritizing the integration and preservation of green spaces, cities can create healthier, more resilient environments that support the well-being of both people and nature. As urban landscapes continue to evolve, the commitment to nurturing these vital green oases will be instrumental in shaping the future of urban living.

Chapter 3: The Healing Power of Plants

Medicinal Plants and Traditional Remedies

Medicinal plants, often revered as nature's pharmacy, have been integral to human health and healing practices for millennia. Across cultures and continents, traditional remedies derived from plants have provided relief from ailments and diseases, shaping the foundation of modern medicine. This rich tapestry of botanical knowledge reflects the deep connection between humans and the natural world, a relationship rooted in observation, experimentation, and tradition.

The journey of medicinal plants begins with the understanding of their active compounds, the chemical constituents responsible for their therapeutic properties. These compounds, which include alkaloids, flavonoids, terpenoids, and glycosides, interact with the human body in various ways, influencing physiological processes and promoting healing. For instance, the bark of the willow tree contains salicin, a precursor to aspirin, which has been used for centuries to alleviate pain and reduce inflammation. Similarly, the leaves of the ginkgo biloba tree are rich in flavonoids and terpenoids, compounds that enhance memory and cognitive function.

Traditional remedies, often passed down through generations, represent a wealth of empirical knowledge about the efficacy and safety of medicinal plants. Indigenous cultures, in particular, have developed sophisticated systems of healing that incorporate plant-based treatments, often in combination with spiritual and cultural practices. The use of medicinal plants in Ayurveda, Traditional Chinese Medicine (TCM), and other indigenous healing systems illustrates the diverse ways in which plants are used therapeutically, addressing not only physical symptoms but also the underlying imbalances in the body and mind.

The integration of medicinal plants into modern healthcare systems has gained momentum as interest in natural and holistic approaches to healing grows. Scientific research has validated many traditional uses of medicinal plants, uncovering their potential to treat a wide range of conditions, from chronic diseases to acute infections. The development of pharmaceuticals often involves the isolation and synthesis of plant-derived compounds, underscoring the importance of botanical knowledge in drug discovery. For example, the anti-cancer drug paclitaxel, derived from the Pacific yew tree, exemplifies how plant compounds can be harnessed to create life-saving treatments.

Cultivating medicinal plants, whether in a home garden or on a larger scale, offers an accessible way to engage with traditional remedies and enhance personal health.

Growing herbs such as peppermint, chamomile, and lavender provides an opportunity to explore their culinary and medicinal uses while fostering a connection to the cycles of nature. These plants can be used to create teas, tinctures, and salves, offering natural solutions for common ailments like digestive issues, stress, and minor skin irritations.

Sustainability is a critical consideration in the use of medicinal plants, particularly as demand for natural remedies increases. Overharvesting and habitat destruction pose significant threats to wild plant populations, endangering both biodiversity and the cultural heritage of communities that rely on these resources. Efforts to promote sustainable harvesting practices, cultivation of medicinal plants, and conservation of natural habitats are essential for ensuring the availability of these valuable resources for future generations. Organizations and initiatives that support the ethical sourcing of medicinal plants play a vital role in protecting both the environment and traditional knowledge.

Education and awareness about the benefits and proper use of medicinal plants are key to integrating traditional remedies into modern health practices safely and effectively. Workshops, courses, and community programs can provide valuable information on identifying, growing, and using medicinal plants, empowering individuals to take an active role in their health. Collaborations between traditional healers, scientists, and healthcare professionals can bridge the gap between ancient wisdom and contemporary medicine, fostering a more holistic approach to health and well-being.

The cultural significance of medicinal plants extends beyond their therapeutic properties, embodying the values, beliefs, and practices of the communities that use them. Rituals and ceremonies involving plants such as sage, cedar, and sweetgrass highlight their role in spiritual cleansing and protection, reflecting a worldview in which health is interconnected with the environment and the cosmos. Preserving the cultural heritage associated with medicinal plants is essential for maintaining the diversity of healing practices and honoring the knowledge of indigenous peoples.

Incorporating medicinal plants into daily life encourages a mindful and intentional approach to health, emphasizing prevention and balance. Simple practices such as drinking herbal teas, using essential oils, and incorporating medicinal herbs into cooking can support physical and emotional well-being, fostering resilience and vitality. By embracing the healing power of plants, individuals can cultivate a deeper connection to nature and a greater sense of harmony within themselves and their surroundings.

The exploration of medicinal plants and traditional remedies reveals a profound legacy of innovation, resilience, and adaptability. As we navigate the complexities of modern health challenges, the wisdom of these age-old practices offers valuable insights and solutions. By honoring and preserving the knowledge of medicinal plants, we can ensure that their benefits continue to enrich our lives and contribute to the health of our planet. Engaging with this legacy inspires a holistic vision of health, one that embraces the interconnectedness of all living things and the potential for healing that lies within the natural world.

Modern Applications of Plant-Based Therapies

The resurgence of interest in plant-based therapies marks a profound shift in contemporary healthcare, as more people turn to nature's pharmacy for holistic healing solutions. This renewed appreciation for the therapeutic potential of plants is not merely a nod to ancient traditions but a recognition of their relevance in addressing modern health challenges. Plant-based therapies encompass a wide spectrum of applications, from dietary supplements and herbal medicines to essential oils and phytotherapy, each contributing to a comprehensive approach to wellness.

Dietary supplements derived from plants have become a staple in many households, offering a convenient way to incorporate beneficial compounds into daily routines. These supplements, which include vitamins, minerals, and herbal extracts, support various aspects of health, such as boosting immunity, improving cognitive function, and promoting cardiovascular wellness. For instance, omega-3 fatty acids, commonly sourced from flaxseeds and algae, are renowned for their anti-inflammatory properties and their role in heart and brain health. Turmeric, with its active compound curcumin, is another popular supplement known for its antioxidant and anti-inflammatory effects, making it a valuable addition to anti-aging and joint health regimens.

Herbal medicines, a cornerstone of plant-based therapies, provide targeted relief for a range of ailments, drawing on centuries of traditional knowledge and modern research. These remedies harness the power of plant compounds to address specific health concerns, often with fewer side effects than synthetic drugs. For example, echinacea is widely used to prevent and treat colds and flu, thanks to its immune-boosting properties. Milk thistle, rich in the compound silymarin, is employed to support liver health and detoxification processes. The use of herbal teas, tinctures, and capsules allows individuals to tailor their treatment to their unique needs, offering a personalized approach to healthcare.

Essential oils, the concentrated aromatic compounds extracted from plants, have gained popularity for their therapeutic applications in aromatherapy and topical treatments. These oils, each with distinct properties, can influence mood, alleviate stress, and promote physical healing. Lavender oil, for instance, is celebrated for its calming effects, aiding in relaxation and sleep. Tea tree oil, known for its antimicrobial properties, is commonly used in skincare to treat acne and infections. The versatility of essential oils allows for their integration into various aspects of daily life, from diffusing to enhance the ambiance of a space to incorporating into personal care products.

Phytotherapy, the use of plant-derived compounds in medicinal practices, bridges the gap between traditional herbal medicine and modern pharmacology. This approach emphasizes the use of whole plant extracts rather than isolated compounds, reflecting the belief that the synergy of multiple constituents enhances therapeutic efficacy. Phytotherapy is employed in the management of chronic conditions, such as diabetes, hypertension, and arthritis, where plant compounds can complement conventional treatments and improve patient outcomes. The growing body of scientific evidence supporting phytotherapy underscores its potential as a legitimate and effective component of modern healthcare.

Integrating plant-based therapies into modern medicine involves a careful balance of tradition and innovation. Research and clinical trials play a crucial role in validating the efficacy and safety of these therapies, ensuring that they meet rigorous standards before being recommended for widespread use. This scientific scrutiny not only enhances the credibility of plant-based treatments but also uncovers new applications and benefits. Collaboration between researchers, healthcare professionals, and traditional healers facilitates the exchange of knowledge and fosters a more holistic approach to health and wellness.

The accessibility and affordability of plant-based therapies contribute to their appeal, offering cost-effective alternatives to conventional treatments. In many parts of the world, these therapies are the primary source of healthcare, providing essential remedies in areas with limited access to pharmaceuticals. The cultivation and harvesting of medicinal plants also support local economies, creating opportunities for sustainable development and empowerment. By prioritizing ethical sourcing and fair trade practices, the plant-based therapy industry can promote social and environmental responsibility.

Education and awareness initiatives are vital for empowering individuals to make informed decisions about their health and the use of plant-based therapies. Workshops, seminars, and online resources provide valuable information on the benefits, preparation, and safe use of these therapies, enabling people to incorporate them into their lifestyles confidently. Healthcare providers, too, play a key role in guiding patients through the integration of plant-based treatments with conventional care, ensuring a cohesive and effective approach to health management.

The environmental implications of plant-based therapies are significant, as they encourage a greater connection to nature and highlight the importance of biodiversity conservation. The sustainable cultivation of medicinal plants relies on the preservation of ecosystems and the careful management of natural resources. Efforts to protect plant habitats and promote biodiversity are essential for maintaining the availability of therapeutic species and safeguarding the ecological balance. By fostering a deeper appreciation for the natural world, plant-based therapies inspire a commitment to environmental stewardship and sustainability.

The exploration of modern applications of plant-based therapies reveals a dynamic and evolving landscape, where tradition meets innovation in the pursuit of health and healing. As we continue to navigate the complexities of modern healthcare, the integration of these therapies offers a promising path toward a more holistic and balanced approach. By embracing the wisdom of nature and harnessing the power of plants, we can enhance our well-being and contribute to a more sustainable and harmonious future. This journey into the realm of plant-based therapies is not just about treating illness but about cultivating a deeper connection with the natural world and rediscovering the healing potential that lies within it.

The Role of Plants in Mental Well-being

The verdant world of plants offers more than just aesthetic pleasure and ecological benefits; it plays a profound role in enhancing mental well-being. The connection between humans and the natural environment is deeply ingrained, a relationship that has been recognized since ancient times. As modern life becomes increasingly fast-paced and stressful, the therapeutic influence of plants on mental health is gaining renewed attention, providing solace and healing in a world that often feels overwhelming.

Gardening, perhaps the most direct interaction with plants, serves as a powerful tool for improving mental well-being. Engaging with soil, nurturing seedlings, and witnessing the growth of plants can be immensely satisfying and calming. This hands-on activity provides a sense of accomplishment and purpose, which can be particularly beneficial for individuals experiencing depression or anxiety. The rhythmic, repetitive tasks involved in gardening, such as planting, weeding, and watering, offer a meditative quality that helps to focus the mind and alleviate stress. Furthermore, exposure to sunlight while gardening boosts serotonin levels, enhancing mood and promoting a sense of well-being.

Indoor plants have emerged as allies in mental health, bringing the benefits of nature into homes and workplaces. These green companions purify the air, increase humidity, and create a soothing atmosphere that fosters relaxation and concentration. Studies have shown that the presence of indoor plants can reduce stress, lower blood pressure, and improve cognitive performance. For those working in office environments, strategically placed plants can enhance creativity, productivity, and overall job satisfaction. The act of caring for indoor plants, even on a small scale, provides a sense of responsibility and connection to nature that can be grounding and restorative.

The concept of biophilia, the innate human affinity for nature, underscores the importance of incorporating natural elements into daily life to support mental health. Incorporating plants into urban environments through green spaces, vertical gardens, and green roofs not only enhances aesthetic appeal but also contributes to psychological and emotional well-being. Access to green spaces has been linked to reduced stress levels, improved mood, and increased social interactions, all of which are vital components of mental well-being. For city dwellers, these natural sanctuaries offer a respite from the concrete and chaos, providing opportunities for exercise, reflection, and rejuvenation.

Beyond their physical presence, plants contribute to mental well-being through their aromatic qualities. Aromatherapy, the use of plant-derived essential oils for therapeutic purposes, harnesses the power of scent to influence mood and emotional health. Essential oils like lavender, chamomile, and bergamot are known for their calming effects, helping to alleviate anxiety, depression, and insomnia. Inhaling these natural fragrances can stimulate the olfactory system and subsequently influence areas of the brain associated with emotions and memories, creating a sense of calm and relaxation.

The sensory experience of being in nature, often referred to as "forest bathing" or shinrin-yoku in Japan, emphasizes the mental health benefits of immersing oneself in a natural environment. This practice encourages individuals to slow down and engage with the natural world through all their senses, promoting mindfulness and reducing stress. The presence of trees, plants, and wildlife creates a multisensory experience that can lower cortisol levels, enhance mood, and improve overall emotional well-being. The simplicity of being surrounded by nature allows for introspection and a break from the constant stimuli of modern life.

For individuals living with mental health conditions, horticultural therapy offers a structured approach to using plants as a therapeutic tool. This form of therapy involves guided activities with plants and gardens to achieve specific therapeutic goals, such as improving social skills, enhancing self-esteem, and fostering a sense of accomplishment. Horticultural therapy has been shown to be effective in diverse settings, from hospitals and rehabilitation centers to schools and community programs, providing a supportive and nurturing environment for healing and growth.

The symbolic and cultural significance of plants also contributes to their role in mental well-being. Throughout history, plants have been used in rituals, ceremonies, and art to convey emotions, commemorate events, and foster spiritual connections. The symbolism of plants, such as the resilience of a cactus or the renewal represented by a blooming flower, can inspire reflection and personal growth. Engaging with plants in this symbolic context offers opportunities for self-expression and emotional exploration, enriching the journey toward mental well-being.

Incorporating plants into mental health practices requires a thoughtful approach that considers individual preferences, needs, and circumstances. For some, cultivating a garden or maintaining indoor plants may be a fulfilling and accessible way to connect with nature. For others, participating in community gardening projects or spending time in local parks might provide the social interaction and sense of belonging that enhances mental well-being. Personalized interventions, guided by mental health professionals, can help individuals harness the therapeutic potential of plants in ways that are meaningful and impactful.

Education and advocacy play crucial roles in promoting the mental health benefits of plants, encouraging individuals and communities to embrace green spaces and nature-based practices. Workshops, public awareness campaigns, and partnerships between mental health organizations and environmental groups can raise awareness and foster a culture of well-being rooted in nature. By highlighting the evidence-based benefits of plants for mental health, these efforts can inspire policy changes and investments in green infrastructure that prioritize mental well-being.

In a world where mental health challenges are increasingly prevalent, the role of plants in fostering mental well-being offers a promising avenue for holistic healing. By integrating plants into our lives, we can cultivate a sense of balance, connection, and peace that supports emotional resilience and enhances the quality of life. The wisdom of nature, embodied in the diverse forms and functions of plants, invites us to explore new pathways to mental well-being, nurturing both our minds and our connection to the natural world. This green journey holds the potential to transform not only individual lives but also the collective health of our communities and the planet.

Aromatherapy and Essential Oils

Aromatherapy, the art and science of using essential oils extracted from plants to enhance physical and mental well-being, has roots stretching back thousands of years. These aromatic oils, carefully distilled from flowers, leaves, bark, and roots, capture the essence of the plants from which they originate, offering a concentrated source of therapeutic benefits. Practitioners and enthusiasts alike have long revered these oils for their ability to soothe the mind, invigorate the body, and promote holistic health.

The allure of essential oils lies in their complex chemical composition, each oil offering a unique blend of compounds that interact with the human body in various ways. These compounds, which include terpenes, esters, alcohols, and ketones, influence the olfactory system and, through it, the limbic system—the part of the brain responsible for emotions, behavior, and long-term memory. This direct pathway to the brain is what makes aromatherapy such a powerful tool for influencing mood and emotional well-being.

Lavender oil, renowned for its calming and relaxing properties, is a staple in aromatherapy. Its delicate floral scent is often used to alleviate anxiety, stress, and insomnia, helping individuals achieve a state of peace and tranquility. The application of lavender oil in a warm bath or as a pillow spray can transform a simple evening routine into a restorative ritual, promoting restful sleep and emotional balance. Similarly, chamomile oil, with its sweet, apple-like aroma, offers soothing effects that are beneficial for relieving nervous tension and encouraging relaxation.

Peppermint oil, with its invigorating and refreshing scent, serves as an effective remedy for mental fatigue and headaches. Its cooling properties provide relief from tension headaches when applied to the temples, while its stimulating aroma can enhance concentration and boost energy levels. Inhaling peppermint oil during a midday slump can offer a natural pick-me-up, invigorating the senses and sharpening focus.

For those seeking to uplift their spirits, citrus oils such as lemon, orange, and bergamot are excellent choices. These oils are celebrated for their cheerful and energizing scents, which can enhance mood and promote a sense of happiness and well-being. Diffusing citrus oils in a living space can create an atmosphere of positivity and vitality, making them ideal for combating feelings of sadness or lethargy.

In addition to their aromatic benefits, essential oils possess antimicrobial, antifungal, and anti-inflammatory properties, making them valuable allies in supporting physical health. Tea tree oil, a potent antimicrobial, is commonly used in skincare to address acne and fungal infections. Its ability to cleanse and purify makes it a popular choice for treating minor cuts and abrasions as well. Eucalyptus oil, known for its decongestant properties, is often used to relieve respiratory conditions such as colds and sinusitis. Inhaling eucalyptus steam or adding a few drops to a humidifier can provide relief from congestion and support respiratory health.

The versatility of essential oils extends beyond personal care to household use, where they offer natural alternatives to chemical-laden products. Essential oils can be used to create homemade cleaning solutions that are both effective and environmentally friendly. A blend of lemon, tea tree, and lavender oils can be used to disinfect surfaces, leaving a fresh, clean scent behind. Similarly, adding a few drops of essential oil to laundry detergent or a cloth dryer ball can infuse clothes with a pleasant fragrance, eliminating the need for synthetic fabric softeners.

To harness the benefits of essential oils safely and effectively, it is important to understand their proper use and application. Essential oils are highly concentrated and should be used with care, often requiring dilution with a carrier oil such as coconut, jojoba, or almond oil before topical application. This dilution not only prevents skin irritation but also helps the skin absorb the oils more effectively. When using essential oils for aromatherapy, a diffuser is a convenient and safe way to disperse the oils into the air, allowing for gentle inhalation of the therapeutic aromas.

For those new to aromatherapy, starting with a few versatile oils and gradually building a collection is a practical approach. Experimenting with different oils and blends can help individuals discover personal preferences and tailor their aromatherapy practices to suit their unique needs. Resources such as books, workshops, and online courses offer valuable information on the properties and uses of essential oils, empowering individuals to make informed choices and enhance their well-being naturally.

While the benefits of aromatherapy and essential oils are numerous, it is important to approach their use with mindfulness and respect for individual sensitivities and health conditions. Consulting with a qualified aromatherapist or healthcare professional can provide guidance on safe and effective use, particularly for individuals with allergies, respiratory conditions, or skin sensitivities. Pregnant and nursing women, as well as individuals with specific health concerns, should seek professional advice before incorporating essential oils into their routines.

As the popularity of aromatherapy continues to grow, the sustainability and ethical sourcing of essential oils have become important considerations. The production of essential oils requires significant plant material, and unsustainable harvesting practices can threaten biodiversity and the health of ecosystems. Supporting companies and producers that prioritize ethical sourcing, fair trade, and environmental stewardship is crucial for ensuring the long-term availability of these precious resources.

Aromatherapy and essential oils offer a natural and holistic approach to enhancing well-being, inviting individuals to explore the therapeutic power of plants. By integrating these aromatic allies into daily life, one can cultivate a greater sense of balance, harmony, and vitality. The journey into the world of essential oils is not just about discovering new scents but about rediscovering the profound connection between nature and health, a connection that has the potential to transform both individuals and communities in meaningful ways. This exploration encourages a deeper appreciation for the gifts of the natural world and the timeless wisdom it holds for nurturing body, mind, and spirit.

Nutritional Benefits of a Plant-Based Diet

The shift toward a plant-based diet is gaining momentum, fueled by growing awareness of its myriad health benefits. Embracing a diet rich in fruits, vegetables, whole grains, nuts, and legumes not only supports personal well-being but also aligns with sustainable and ethical food practices. The nutritional advantages of a plant-based diet are comprehensive, offering a wealth of vitamins, minerals, antioxidants, and fiber that contribute to optimal health and vitality.

At the heart of a plant-based diet is the abundance of essential nutrients that are often less prevalent in diets heavy in animal products. Fruits and vegetables are powerhouses of vitamins and minerals, providing nutrients such as vitamin C, potassium, folate, and beta-carotene. These nutrients play critical roles in maintaining healthy skin, boosting immune function, and supporting cellular repair and growth. For instance, leafy greens like spinach and kale are rich in calcium and magnesium, essential for bone health and muscle function.

Fiber, a key component of plant-based foods, is instrumental in promoting digestive health. Unlike animal products, plant foods are naturally high in fiber, which aids in regular bowel movements and prevents constipation. A diet high in fiber has also been associated with a reduced risk of chronic diseases such as heart disease, type 2 diabetes, and certain cancers. Soluble fiber found in foods like oats, beans, and fruits can help lower blood cholesterol levels, while insoluble fiber from whole grains and vegetables adds bulk to the diet and aids in satiety, helping to manage weight.

Antioxidants, abundant in a plant-based diet, are compounds that protect the body from oxidative stress and inflammation, which are linked to the development of chronic diseases. Foods rich in antioxidants, such as berries, nuts, and dark chocolate, neutralize harmful free radicals and contribute to the prevention of heart disease, cancer, and neurodegenerative disorders. The vibrant colors of fruits and vegetables often indicate the presence of specific antioxidants, such as lycopene in tomatoes and anthocyanins in blueberries, each offering unique health benefits.

Protein, often a concern for those transitioning to a plant-based diet, is readily available from a variety of plant sources. Legumes, such as lentils, chickpeas, and black beans, are excellent sources of protein, providing essential amino acids needed for muscle repair and growth. Nuts and seeds, including almonds, chia seeds, and hemp seeds, are also rich in protein and healthy fats, supporting heart health and providing long-lasting energy. Incorporating a diverse range of plant proteins ensures an adequate intake of all essential amino acids, comparable to those found in animal products.

The inclusion of healthy fats in a plant-based diet is crucial for maintaining heart health and supporting brain function. Foods like avocados, olives, and walnuts are rich in monounsaturated and polyunsaturated fats, which help reduce bad cholesterol levels and lower the risk of heart disease. Omega-3 fatty acids, found in flaxseeds, chia seeds, and algae, play a vital role in brain health, reducing inflammation, and supporting cognitive function. These healthy fats also contribute to the absorption of fat-soluble vitamins, such as vitamins A, D, E, and K, enhancing overall nutrient utilization.

A plant-based diet naturally encourages a reduction in the intake of saturated fats and cholesterol, often found in animal products. This shift can lead to improved heart health, as lower levels of saturated fats and cholesterol are associated with reduced blood pressure and a lower risk of heart disease. Additionally, plant-based diets tend to be lower in calories, which can aid in weight management and reduce the risk of obesity-related conditions.

Transitioning to a plant-based diet offers the opportunity to explore a diverse array of foods and flavors, encouraging culinary creativity and exploration. The variety of plant-based options available means that meals can be both nutritious and delicious, with countless recipes and cuisines to discover. Experimenting with different cooking methods, spices, and herbs can transform simple ingredients into satisfying and flavorful dishes that cater to all taste preferences.

For those new to a plant-based lifestyle, gradual changes can ease the transition and make it more sustainable in the long term. Starting with "Meatless Mondays" or incorporating more plant-based meals throughout the week can help individuals adjust to new foods and flavors without feeling overwhelmed. Planning meals and stocking the pantry with plant-based staples, such as whole grains, legumes, nuts, seeds, and fresh produce, ensures that nutritious options are always available.

While a plant-based diet offers numerous health benefits, it is important to ensure that it is balanced and provides all necessary nutrients. Vitamin B12, primarily found in animal products, may require supplementation or consumption of fortified foods for those on a strict plant-based diet. Similarly, attention should be given to obtaining adequate iron, zinc, and calcium, which can be sourced from fortified cereals, leafy greens, and legumes, or supplemented as needed.

The environmental benefits of a plant-based diet further underscore its appeal, as plant-based foods generally have a lower carbon footprint and require fewer natural resources than animal-based foods. This dietary change contributes to the reduction of greenhouse gas emissions, deforestation, and water usage, aligning personal health goals with global sustainability efforts.

The nutritional benefits of a plant-based diet extend beyond individual health, fostering a deeper connection to food, the environment, and community. By choosing plant-based options, individuals can take active steps toward improving their health, supporting ethical food practices, and contributing to a more sustainable future. This dietary shift, rooted in the abundance and diversity of the plant kingdom, invites a holistic approach to well-being, embracing the interconnectedness of health, nature, and lifestyle. As more people discover the joy and vitality of a plant-based diet, the collective impact on personal and planetary health becomes increasingly significant, paving the way for a healthier, more compassionate world.

Chapter 4: Plants in Culture and Society

The Symbolic Use of Plants in Different Cultures

Throughout history, plants have transcended their roles as mere sources of sustenance and aesthetics to become powerful symbols embedded in the cultural fabric of societies across the globe. Their presence in mythology, religion, and folklore reflects a rich tapestry of human beliefs and values, offering insight into the ways in which people have connected with nature and imbued it with meaning. As symbols, plants have conveyed messages of life, death, rebirth, and transformation, each culture interpreting them through a unique lens shaped by its environment and history.

In ancient Egypt, the lotus flower held profound significance, symbolizing the cycle of life, death, and rebirth. As a plant that rises from the muddy waters to bloom in the sun, the lotus represented purity and enlightenment, themes that resonated deeply with Egyptian beliefs about the afterlife. The lotus was often depicted in art and architecture, adorning the capitals of columns and the walls of temples, serving as a reminder of the eternal nature of the human soul. This symbolism was so integral to Egyptian culture that the lotus became associated with the sun god Ra, further emphasizing its connection to creation and renewal.

Similarly, in Hinduism and Buddhism, the lotus is revered as a symbol of spiritual awakening and divine beauty. In Hindu mythology, the god Vishnu is often depicted resting on a lotus, while the goddess Lakshmi emerges from one, signifying prosperity and enlightenment. In Buddhism, the lotus is a metaphor for the purity of the mind, which remains untouched by the murky waters of desire and attachment. The image of the Buddha seated on a lotus throne reinforces the idea of spiritual transcendence and the journey toward enlightenment.

In ancient Greece, plants played a central role in mythology and religious practices. The olive tree, sacred to the goddess Athena, symbolized peace, wisdom, and victory. According to legend, Athena gifted the olive tree to the people of Athens, bestowing prosperity and nourishment upon the city. The olive branch became a universal emblem of peace, a tradition that endures to this day. The laurel tree, associated with Apollo, was a symbol of victory and achievement, its leaves used to crown victors in athletic competitions and poetic contests. The enduring legacy of these symbols reflects the Greeks' reverence for nature and its ability to convey divine messages.

In Chinese culture, plants are imbued with symbolic meanings that permeate art, literature, and daily life. The bamboo, with its strength and flexibility, represents resilience and integrity, qualities highly valued in Chinese philosophy. Its ability to bend without breaking is seen as a metaphor for adaptability and perseverance in the face of adversity. The plum blossom, blooming in the harshness of winter, symbolizes courage and hope, reminding people of the promise of renewal and the beauty of endurance. These plants, among others, are celebrated in Chinese poetry and painting, their symbolism providing inspiration and guidance.

In the Celtic tradition, trees held sacred status, revered as living entities with spiritual significance. The Druids, ancient Celtic priests, believed that trees were the homes of deities and spirits, each species embodying specific virtues and powers. The oak tree, a symbol of strength and endurance, was considered the king of the forest, often associated with thunder gods and used in rituals to invoke protection and wisdom. The yew tree, with its long lifespan and evergreen nature, symbolized death and rebirth, serving as a link between the physical and spiritual worlds. These beliefs were intricately woven into Celtic myths and rituals, reflecting a deep connection with the natural world.

In Native American cultures, plants are seen as vital components of the web of life, each species possessing unique qualities and teachings. The corn plant, known as maize, holds a central place in many indigenous cultures, symbolizing sustenance, fertility, and community. As a staple crop, corn is celebrated in ceremonies and dances, its cultivation intertwined with spiritual practices and seasonal cycles. Tobacco, considered a sacred plant, is used in rituals and offerings to communicate with the spirit world, its smoke carrying prayers and intentions. These symbolic uses of plants underscore the interconnectedness of life and the respect for nature that is fundamental to indigenous worldviews.

The symbolic use of plants is not limited to ancient cultures; it continues to evolve and resonate in contemporary societies. In Western culture, the red rose is a widely recognized symbol of love and passion, often exchanged as a token of affection on special occasions. The language of flowers, known as floriography, emerged in the Victorian era, allowing people to convey emotions and messages through floral arrangements. Each flower carried a specific meaning, enabling subtle communication in a time of strict social conventions.

In Japan, the cherry blossom, or sakura, is a national symbol of beauty and transience. The fleeting nature of the cherry blossom season, with its brief yet spectacular bloom, serves as a reminder of the impermanence of life and the value of appreciating the present moment. Hanami, the tradition of viewing cherry blossoms, is a cherished cultural event that brings people together to celebrate the arrival of spring and reflect on the passage of time.

The symbolic use of plants offers a window into the values and beliefs of different cultures, highlighting the universal human desire to find meaning and connection in the natural world. These symbols transcend language and geography, speaking to shared experiences of growth, transformation, and renewal. By exploring the symbolic significance of plants, we gain insight into the diverse ways in which people have sought to understand their place in the world and their relationship with nature.

In a modern context, the symbolic use of plants continues to inspire art, literature, and design, bridging the gap between tradition and innovation. As we navigate complex global challenges, the timeless wisdom embodied in plant symbolism offers guidance and hope, reminding us of the resilience and beauty inherent in the natural world. By honoring these symbols and the cultural heritage they represent, we celebrate the rich tapestry of human expression and our enduring connection to the earth. This exploration of plant symbolism invites us to reflect on our own values and aspirations, fostering a deeper appreciation for the living world and the stories it holds.

Plants in Art and Literature

From the earliest cave paintings to contemporary installations, plants have held a prominent place in the world of art and literature. They serve as both subjects and symbols, capturing the imagination of artists and writers throughout history. The depiction of plants in creative works reflects the human desire to interpret and connect with the natural world, offering insights into cultural values, personal expression, and the intricate relationship between humans and the environment.

Art has long utilized plants as a central motif, their forms and colors providing endless inspiration for artistic expression. The lush foliage of a tree, the delicate petals of a flower, or the intricate patterns of leaves have found their way onto countless canvases, each brushstroke capturing the beauty and complexity of the natural world. In ancient times, plants were often depicted in religious and mythological contexts, serving as symbols of fertility, life, and divine connection. Egyptian wall paintings frequently featured papyrus and lotus motifs, while Greek vases and frescoes depicted olive branches and laurel wreaths as emblems of victory and peace.

The Renaissance period witnessed a renewed interest in the natural world, with artists like Leonardo da Vinci and Albrecht Dürer producing detailed botanical studies that merged scientific observation with artistic skill. These works not only celebrated the beauty of plants but also contributed to the burgeoning field of botany, capturing the structure and intricacies of plant life with unprecedented accuracy. The botanical illustrations of this era remain valuable resources for both artists and scientists, bridging the gap between art and science.

The Impressionist movement of the 19th century further embraced the beauty of plants, with artists like Claude

Monet and Pierre-Auguste Renoir capturing the ephemeral qualities of light and color in nature. Monet's series of water lilies and his garden at Giverny are iconic examples of how plants can evoke mood and emotion, transforming simple garden scenes into masterpieces of atmospheric beauty. The Impressionists' focus on capturing the fleeting moments of nature continues to influence artists today, inspiring them to explore the harmonious interplay between light, color, and form.

In literature, plants have served as powerful symbols and metaphors, enriching narratives with layers of meaning. Shakespeare's plays and sonnets are replete with botanical references, using flowers and herbs to convey themes of love, jealousy, and mortality. In "A Midsummer Night's Dream," the use of a magical flower to manipulate love highlights the enchanting and unpredictable nature of emotions. Similarly, in "Hamlet," Ophelia's distribution of symbolic flowers reflects her descent into madness and the chaos surrounding her.

The Romantic poets, captivated by the sublime beauty of nature, often employed plant imagery to explore themes of transcendence, spirituality, and the human condition. Wordsworth's "I Wandered Lonely as a Cloud" immortalizes the daffodil as a symbol of natural beauty and emotional solace, while Keats' "Ode to a Nightingale" uses the nightingale and its woodland habitat to express longing and the ephemeral nature of life. These works underscore the Romantic belief in the restorative power of nature and its ability to inspire introspection and creative expression.

In contemporary literature, plants continue to play a significant role, often serving as metaphors for personal growth, resilience, and environmental awareness. In Barbara Kingsolver's "The Poisonwood Bible," the lush Congolese landscape mirrors the complexities of cultural and familial dynamics, highlighting the interconnectedness of people and place. Similarly, in Richard Powers' "The Overstory," trees become central characters, their lives and stories intertwining with those of the human protagonists to illuminate themes of interdependence and ecological stewardship.

Beyond their symbolic significance, plants are integral to the setting and atmosphere of literary works, shaping the tone and mood of narratives. In Gabriel Garcia Marquez's "One Hundred Years of Solitude," the fictional town of Macondo is brought to life through vivid descriptions of its tropical flora, creating a rich and immersive backdrop for the novel's magical realism. The ever-present nature of the jungle in Joseph Conrad's "Heart of Darkness" serves as both a physical and psychological landscape, reflecting the protagonist's journey into the depths of human nature.

The use of plants in art and literature extends beyond traditional forms, influencing contemporary practices and mediums. Installations and land art often incorporate living plants as dynamic elements, engaging with themes of growth, decay, and environmental change. Artists like

Andy Goldsworthy and Olafur Eliasson use natural materials to create works that explore the transient and cyclical nature of life, inviting viewers to consider their relationship with the environment.

In digital and conceptual art, the symbolism of plants continues to evolve, reflecting contemporary concerns about sustainability, climate change, and biodiversity. Artists and writers use plants to challenge perceptions, provoke dialogue, and inspire action, highlighting the urgent need for environmental consciousness and stewardship. By incorporating plants into their work, they remind audiences of the beauty and vulnerability of the natural world, encouraging a deeper appreciation and responsibility for its preservation.

The enduring presence of plants in art and literature speaks to their universal appeal and capacity to inspire creativity and reflection. As symbols, subjects, and settings, plants offer a wealth of possibilities for artistic and literary exploration, enriching our understanding of the world and our place within it. Through their depiction in creative works, plants become conduits for expression and connection, bridging the gap between humanity and nature, the ephemeral and the eternal. This exploration of plants in art and literature invites us to engage with the natural world in new and meaningful ways, fostering a deeper appreciation for the beauty and complexity that surrounds us.

The Influence of Flora on Human Creativity

Flora, with its abundant diversity and intricate beauty, has long served as a wellspring of inspiration for human creativity. The natural world, teeming with vibrant colors, unique shapes, and complex patterns, offers a limitless palette from which artists, writers, and innovators draw. This innate connection between flora and creativity is evident across cultures and eras, reflecting a profound relationship that continues to inspire and influence human expression.

The visual allure of plants has captivated artists for centuries, prompting them to capture the essence of nature through their work. The vibrant hues of a sunflower field, the delicate symmetry of a fern leaf, or the ethereal glow of a moonlit garden have all found their way onto canvases, each stroke echoing the rhythm of nature. The Impressionist movement, for instance, emerged from the desire to capture the fleeting moments of light and color in nature. Artists like Claude Monet and Vincent van Gogh immersed themselves in gardens and fields, their works a testament to the emotive power of flora. Monet's water lilies, with their dreamy reflections and soft palettes, evoke a serene contemplation of nature, while van Gogh's sunflowers burst with energy and life, reflecting his passionate engagement with the natural world.

In literature, plants often serve as powerful metaphors and symbols, enriching narratives with layers of meaning.

The language of flowers, or floriography, flourished in the Victorian era, allowing writers to convey complex emotions and messages through floral imagery. Each bloom carried its own meaning, enabling subtle communication in a time of strict social conventions. This symbolic use of plants is evident in works by authors such as Emily Dickinson, whose poetry often weaves nature into reflections on life, death, and the human experience. Her use of the daisy and the rose, for instance, evokes themes of innocence and love, inviting readers to explore the depth of human emotion.

Beyond the arts, the influence of flora extends to the realms of science and innovation. The intricate designs found in nature have inspired technological advancements and architectural marvels, a concept known as biomimicry. The study of plants and their adaptive strategies has led to breakthroughs in sustainable design and engineering. The structure of a lotus leaf, with its self-cleaning properties, has inspired the development of water-repellent surfaces. Similarly, the efficient way in which trees transport water has informed the design of energy-efficient buildings and systems. These innovations, rooted in the observation of natural processes, highlight the potential for flora to inspire solutions to contemporary challenges.

The symbiotic relationship between plants and creativity is also evident in the culinary arts, where chefs draw inspiration from the flavors, textures, and colors of nature. The farm-to-table movement emphasizes the use of fresh, locally sourced ingredients, celebrating the diversity and richness of plant-based foods. Chefs experiment with herbs, fruits, and vegetables, transforming them into artful dishes that engage the senses and tell a story of seasonality and terroir. This culinary creativity not only delights the palate but also fosters a deeper appreciation for the connection between nature and nourishment.

Gardening, as both an art form and a therapeutic practice, embodies the creative potential inherent in working with flora. The act of designing and tending a garden allows for personal expression and reflection, offering a canvas on which to explore color, form, and texture. Gardeners, much like artists, compose with living elements, creating spaces that evoke beauty, tranquility, and joy. The process of nurturing plants and witnessing their growth fosters a sense of connection and mindfulness, enhancing well-being and inspiring creativity in other areas of life.

The influence of flora on human creativity is not limited to individual expression; it also plays a role in shaping cultural identity and collective imagination. The symbolic use of plants in rituals, myths, and traditions reveals the deep-rooted connections between communities and their natural surroundings. In many indigenous cultures, plants are revered as sacred entities, their stories and uses passed down through generations. These cultural narratives, rich with botanical knowledge, continue to inspire contemporary artists and writers, preserving the wisdom and beauty of ancestral practices.

In urban environments, the presence of flora offers a vital connection to nature, fostering creativity and well-being. Green spaces, from parks to botanical gardens, provide refuge from the hustle and bustle of city life, inviting contemplation and inspiration. The integration of plants into urban design, through initiatives such as green roofs and vertical gardens, enhances the aesthetic and environmental quality of cities, encouraging a harmonious relationship between nature and human habitation.

As we look to the future, the influence of flora on creativity continues to evolve, offering new possibilities for expression and innovation. Advances in technology and science, coupled with an increasing awareness of environmental sustainability, invite a reimagining of our relationship with the natural world. Artists and creators are exploring new mediums and collaborations, blending nature with digital and interactive elements to create immersive experiences that challenge and inspire.

The enduring presence of flora in human creativity speaks to its universal appeal and its capacity to evoke wonder and imagination. Plants, in their infinite variety and complexity, offer a source of inspiration that transcends boundaries, inviting us to explore the interconnectedness of life and the beauty that surrounds us. By engaging with flora, we not only enrich our creative endeavors but also deepen our understanding of the world and our place within it. This exploration of the influence of plants on creativity invites us to celebrate the natural world and embrace the limitless potential it holds for inspiring and transforming human expression.

Rituals and Traditions Involving Plants

Across the globe, rituals and traditions involving plants form an integral part of cultural identities, weaving a rich tapestry of meaning and symbolism that transcends generations. These practices, deeply rooted in history and spirituality, reveal the profound relationship between humans and the natural world. From sacred ceremonies to seasonal celebrations, plants play a pivotal role in marking significant life events, conveying messages, and maintaining a connection to the environment.

One of the most enduring plant-based traditions is the use of incense in religious and spiritual rituals. Incense, made from the resin of aromatic plants, has been used for thousands of years in cultures such as those in Egypt, India, and China. The act of burning incense is believed to purify the air, create a sacred atmosphere, and facilitate communication with the divine. In Hinduism, incense is offered to deities during puja ceremonies, while in Buddhism, it accompanies meditation and prayer, symbolizing the transience of life. The fragrant smoke of incense serves as a bridge between the physical and spiritual realms, enhancing the ritual experience and fostering a sense of peace and mindfulness.

In many indigenous cultures, plants are revered as sacred entities, integral to rituals that honor the interconnectedness of life. The use of tobacco in Native American ceremonies exemplifies this reverence. Tobacco is considered a sacred plant, its smoke carrying prayers and intentions to the spirit world. It is used in ceremonies to seek guidance, express gratitude, and establish harmony with nature. Similarly, the ayahuasca vine is central to the spiritual practices of indigenous Amazonian tribes. The brew made from this plant is used in healing ceremonies and spiritual journeys, facilitating introspection and connection with the natural world.

Seasonal celebrations often incorporate plants to mark changes in the natural world and the cycles of life. In Japan, the cherry blossom festival, or Hanami, is a cherished tradition that celebrates the fleeting beauty of sakura blossoms. Families and friends gather under the blooming trees to enjoy picnics and reflect on the impermanence of life. This tradition fosters a sense of community and appreciation for the transient beauty of nature. In Europe, the harvest festival is a time-honored tradition that dates back to ancient times. Celebrated in various forms, from the British Harvest Festival to Germany's Oktoberfest, these events honor the bounty of the earth and express gratitude for the harvest. The use of cornucopias, wheat sheaves, and other plant symbols reinforces the connection between people and the land.

Rituals involving plants also play a significant role in personal and communal life events. In many cultures, weddings incorporate plant symbols to convey blessings and good fortune. The use of floral garlands in Indian weddings, for example, represents love and unity, with the bride and groom exchanging garlands to signify their mutual respect and commitment. In Western cultures, the bridal bouquet, often composed of symbolic flowers, is a traditional element that adds beauty and meaning to the ceremony. The tossing of the bouquet, a custom that dates back to ancient times, is believed to bring good luck to the recipient.

Funerary traditions often include plants as symbols of remembrance and renewal. In many cultures, flowers are placed on graves or used in funeral arrangements to honor the deceased and offer comfort to the bereaved. The use of the white lily in Christian funerals, for example, symbolizes the resurrection and purity of the soul. In Mexico, the Day of the Dead celebration incorporates marigolds, known as "flowers of the dead," to guide spirits to their families and honor the memory of loved ones. These floral tributes serve as a reminder of the cyclical nature of life and the enduring connection between the living and the deceased.

The use of plants in healing rituals highlights their role as sources of physical and spiritual nourishment. Traditional medicine systems, such as Ayurveda and Traditional Chinese Medicine, incorporate a vast array of herbs and plants to restore balance and promote health. These practices are deeply rooted in the belief that plants possess inherent healing properties, reflecting an understanding of the symbiotic relationship between humans and nature. The preparation and use of plant-based remedies are often accompanied by rituals that honor the plants' spirit and enhance their efficacy.

Plants also play a role in rites of passage, marking significant transitions in an individual's life. In some African cultures, initiation ceremonies incorporate plant-based symbols and rituals to signify the transition from childhood to adulthood. These ceremonies often include the use of sacred plants, such as the baobab tree, which represents strength and resilience. The inclusion of plants in these rites underscores their importance as symbols of growth, transformation, and continuity.

In contemporary society, the resurgence of interest in plant-based rituals reflects a desire to reconnect with nature and embrace holistic practices. The popularity of practices such as forest bathing, herbalism, and gardening underscores the therapeutic benefits of interacting with plants and the natural environment. These modern rituals draw on ancient traditions, offering opportunities for personal reflection, healing, and spiritual growth.

The diverse array of rituals and traditions involving plants highlights their significance as symbols of life, transformation, and interconnectedness. These practices, rooted in cultural heritage and spiritual beliefs, offer insights into the ways in which humans have sought to understand and honor the natural world. By participating in these rituals, individuals and communities nurture a sense of belonging and connection, fostering a deeper appreciation for the beauty and wisdom of nature. As we continue to engage with plant-based traditions, we uphold the legacy of our ancestors and celebrate the enduring bond between humanity and the natural world.

The Role of Plants in Sustainable Practices

The increasing global awareness of environmental issues has brought the role of plants in sustainable practices to the forefront of public consciousness. As humanity grapples with the challenges of climate change, resource depletion, and habitat loss, plants offer viable solutions that are both innovative and time-tested. Harnessing the power of plants for sustainable practices not only addresses immediate ecological concerns but also fosters long-term environmental stewardship and resilience.

One of the most significant contributions of plants to sustainability is their ability to mitigate climate change through carbon sequestration. Trees and other vegetation absorb carbon dioxide from the atmosphere, storing carbon within their biomass and releasing oxygen through photosynthesis. This process helps to reduce the concentration of greenhouse gases, which are a major driver of global warming. Forests, in particular, play a critical role in this process, acting as carbon sinks that absorb vast amounts of carbon dioxide. Efforts to preserve and restore forests, such as reforestation and afforestation initiatives, have gained momentum as effective strategies for combating climate change.

Urban environments, with their dense populations and high levels of pollution, also benefit from the incorporation of plants into sustainable practices. Green infrastructure, such as green roofs, vertical gardens, and urban forests, enhances the quality of urban life by improving air quality, reducing heat island effects, and increasing biodiversity. These living systems not only provide ecological benefits but also create aesthetically pleasing spaces that promote well-being and social cohesion. The integration of plants into urban design represents a shift toward more sustainable and livable cities, where nature and human development coexist harmoniously.

Agriculture, a sector heavily reliant on natural resources, is undergoing a transformation as sustainable practices become increasingly essential. Traditional agricultural methods, which often involve monocultures and chemical inputs, have led to soil degradation, water scarcity, and loss of biodiversity. In response, sustainable agriculture emphasizes practices that mimic natural ecosystems, such as agroforestry, permaculture, and organic farming. These methods leverage the benefits of plants to enhance soil fertility, conserve water, and support diverse ecosystems. By fostering a symbiotic relationship between plants and the environment, sustainable agriculture promotes food security while reducing the ecological footprint of farming.

The role of plants in water management is another critical aspect of sustainable practices. Wetlands, mangroves, and riparian buffers serve as natural water filtration systems, removing pollutants and sediments from water bodies. These plant-based ecosystems also act as buffers against flooding and erosion, protecting coastal and riverine communities from extreme weather events. Restoring and preserving these vital ecosystems is essential for maintaining water quality and resilience in the face of climate change. Additionally, the use of constructed wetlands and phytoremediation—where plants are used to clean contaminated soils and water—demonstrates the potential of plants to address environmental pollution and degradation.

In the realm of energy, plants offer promising alternatives to fossil fuels through the production of bioenergy. Biofuels, derived from plant materials such as corn, sugarcane, and algae, provide a renewable source of energy that can reduce dependence on non-renewable resources and decrease greenhouse gas emissions. The development of advanced biofuels, which utilize non-food biomass and agricultural residues, aims to enhance the sustainability and efficiency of bioenergy production. By harnessing the energy stored in plants, bioenergy contributes to a diversified and sustainable energy portfolio.

Biodiversity conservation is intrinsically linked to sustainable practices, with plants playing a central role in maintaining ecosystem health and resilience. Diverse plant communities support a wide range of species, providing habitat, food, and resources for wildlife. Conservation efforts, such as the establishment of protected areas and the restoration of degraded habitats, prioritize the preservation of plant diversity as a means of safeguarding ecosystems and the services they provide. By recognizing the interconnectedness of all living organisms, sustainable practices promote a holistic approach to conservation that values the intrinsic worth of plant life.

The cultural and medicinal value of plants further underscores their importance in sustainable practices. Traditional knowledge systems, which have long recognized the healing properties of plants, offer valuable insights into sustainable resource use and management. The preservation of this knowledge, alongside scientific research and innovation, contributes to the development of sustainable healthcare solutions and the conservation of plant genetic resources. By honoring the cultural significance of plants, sustainable practices acknowledge the diverse ways in which human well-being is intertwined with the natural world.

Education and community engagement are vital components of promoting sustainable practices involving plants. By fostering a deeper understanding of the ecological and economic benefits of plants, educational initiatives empower individuals and communities to take action toward sustainability. Community gardens, tree planting programs, and citizen science projects provide hands-on opportunities for people to connect with nature and contribute to environmental stewardship. These initiatives not only enhance local ecosystems but also build social capital and resilience, creating a sense of shared responsibility for the environment.

The role of plants in sustainable practices is multifaceted, encompassing ecological, economic, and social dimensions. By leveraging the natural processes and benefits of plants, sustainable practices offer solutions to pressing environmental challenges while fostering a harmonious relationship between humans and the natural world. As we continue to explore and implement plant-based strategies, we pave the way for a more sustainable and equitable future, where the well-being of people and the planet are inextricably linked. This commitment to sustainability invites us to reimagine our relationship with nature and embrace the potential of plants to inspire and guide us toward a more sustainable world.

Chapter 5: Economic Contributions of Plants

Agriculture and Crop Production

Agriculture, the cornerstone of human civilization, has evolved over millennia from simple foraging to complex systems of crop production that feed billions. The journey from ancient practices to modern agricultural innovations reflects humanity's ingenuity in harnessing the power of nature to sustain and nourish. Understanding the intricacies of agriculture and crop production is not only essential for feeding a growing population but also for fostering sustainable practices that ensure the health of our planet.

At its core, agriculture revolves around the cultivation of plants for food, fiber, and other essential resources. This process begins with understanding the unique requirements of different crops, including climate, soil, water, and nutrients. Each plant species has specific needs, and successful crop production hinges on meeting these conditions. The art and science of agriculture involve selecting the right crops for the environment, optimizing growing conditions, and managing resources efficiently.

One of the fundamental aspects of crop production is soil management. Healthy soil is the bedrock of agriculture, providing plants with the nutrients, water, and support they need to thrive. Soil fertility depends on its composition, structure, and biological activity. Farmers and agriculturalists employ various techniques to maintain and enhance soil health, such as crop rotation, cover cropping, and the use of organic amendments. Crop rotation involves alternating different crops in a sequence to prevent nutrient depletion and reduce pest and disease buildup. Cover crops, grown between main crops, help prevent erosion, improve soil structure, and enhance nutrient availability. Organic amendments, such as compost and manure, enrich the soil with essential nutrients and improve its physical properties.

Water management is another critical component of successful crop production. Different crops have varying water requirements, and efficient irrigation practices are essential to meet these needs while conserving water resources. Techniques such as drip irrigation, which delivers water directly to the plant roots, reduce water wastage and increase efficiency. Rainwater harvesting and the use of drought-resistant crop varieties further enhance water management, ensuring that crops receive adequate moisture even in challenging conditions.

Pest and disease management is a constant challenge in agriculture, as plants are susceptible to a wide range of insects, pathogens, and weeds. Integrated Pest Management (IPM) offers a holistic approach to managing these threats by combining biological, cultural, mechanical, and chemical methods. IPM emphasizes prevention and monitoring, using natural predators, crop rotation, and resistant varieties to reduce pest populations. When necessary, targeted chemical interventions are employed to minimize environmental impact. This approach not only protects crops but also promotes biodiversity and ecological balance.

The selection of crop varieties is a crucial decision that influences the success of agricultural endeavors. Plant breeding and genetic research have led to the development of high-yielding, disease-resistant, and climate-adapted crop varieties. These advancements enable farmers to cultivate crops that are better suited to their specific environments and challenges. The use of hybrid seeds, which combine desirable traits from different plant lines, has revolutionized crop production, leading to increased yields and improved resilience.

Sustainable agriculture practices are gaining traction as awareness of environmental issues grows. These practices aim to balance productivity with ecological and social responsibility. Agroecology, for example, integrates ecological principles into agricultural systems, promoting biodiversity, soil health, and water conservation. Organic farming, which avoids synthetic inputs and emphasizes natural processes, is another approach that aligns with sustainability goals. By reducing reliance on chemical fertilizers and pesticides, organic farming enhances soil fertility and reduces environmental pollution.

Another promising avenue in sustainable agriculture is the incorporation of technology and innovation. Precision agriculture utilizes data and technology to optimize farming practices, from planting and irrigation to harvesting and pest management. Drones, sensors, and satellite imagery provide real-time information that enables farmers to make informed decisions, reducing waste and increasing efficiency. Vertical farming and hydroponics offer innovative solutions for urban agriculture, allowing for year-round crop production in controlled environments. These technologies not only maximize space and resources but also minimize the impact on traditional farmlands.

Education and knowledge sharing are vital components of advancing agriculture and crop production. Farmers, researchers, and policymakers must collaborate to develop and implement best practices that address local and global challenges. Extension services, farmer cooperatives, and agricultural education programs play a crucial role in disseminating information and fostering innovation. By empowering communities with knowledge and resources, these initiatives contribute to the resilience and sustainability of agricultural systems.

Agriculture is not without its challenges, and addressing them requires a multifaceted approach. Climate change, for instance, poses significant threats to crop production, with extreme weather events, shifting growing seasons, and increased pest pressures. Adapting to these changes involves developing climate-resilient crop varieties, improving water and soil management, and diversifying agricultural systems. Additionally, addressing issues of food security and equity is essential to ensure that all people have access to sufficient, nutritious, and culturally appropriate food.

The journey of agriculture and crop production is one of innovation, adaptation, and interconnectedness. By harnessing the power of plants and the knowledge of generations, agriculture continues to evolve, meeting the needs of a growing population while stewarding the planet's resources. As we look to the future, embracing sustainable practices, technological advancements, and collaborative efforts will be key to fostering a resilient and equitable agricultural system. This ongoing endeavor invites us to reimagine our relationship with the land, honoring the legacy of those who have cultivated before us and nurturing the potential of the fields that sustain us.

Forestry and Renewable Resources

Forestry, a critical component of environmental stewardship, plays a vital role in the sustainable management of renewable resources. As the world grapples with the challenges of deforestation, habitat loss, and climate change, the practice of forestry emerges as a beacon of hope for balancing ecological integrity with human needs. This intricate field encompasses the management, conservation, and sustainable use of forests and their resources, offering a pathway to a more harmonious coexistence with our natural environment.

Forests, vast reservoirs of biodiversity and ecological services, provide a wealth of renewable resources that have supported human societies for millennia. Timber, perhaps the most recognizable resource, is harvested for construction, paper production, and countless other uses. The sustainable management of timber resources ensures that forests can continue to provide these materials without compromising their ecological health. Techniques such as selective logging, which involves harvesting only certain trees while leaving others intact, help maintain forest structure and biodiversity. By allowing forests to regenerate naturally, these practices ensure a continuous supply of timber and other forest products.

Beyond timber, forests offer a myriad of non-timber forest products (NTFPs) that contribute to livelihoods and economies worldwide. These include fruits, nuts, resins, medicinal plants, and fibers, all of which can be harvested sustainably to support local communities. The collection and sale of NTFPs often provide critical income for indigenous and rural populations, fostering economic development while encouraging the conservation of forest ecosystems. Sustainable harvesting practices, such as rotational harvesting and community-based management, empower local communities to manage their resources effectively and equitably.

Forests also play a crucial role in regulating the global climate through carbon sequestration. By absorbing carbon dioxide during photosynthesis, trees act as carbon sinks, mitigating the impacts of greenhouse gas emissions. This process underscores the importance of preserving existing forests and restoring degraded ones as a strategy for combating climate change. Reforestation and afforestation initiatives, which involve planting trees in deforested or non-forested areas, contribute to carbon sequestration, enhance biodiversity, and improve soil and water quality.

The management of renewable resources through sustainable forestry practices requires a comprehensive understanding of ecological processes and human impacts. Forest management plans, tailored to specific regions and ecosystems, guide the sustainable use of forest resources while balancing ecological, economic, and social objectives. These plans often incorporate principles of adaptive management, which involve monitoring forest conditions, evaluating management outcomes, and adjusting practices as needed to achieve desired goals. By fostering a dynamic and responsive approach to forest management, adaptive management ensures that forestry practices remain effective and sustainable in the face of changing environmental conditions.

Community involvement is a cornerstone of successful forestry and renewable resource management. Engaging local communities in the planning and implementation of forestry projects fosters a sense of ownership and responsibility, leading to more effective conservation and resource management outcomes. Community-based forestry initiatives, which empower local populations to manage and benefit from forest resources, have gained recognition as a model for sustainable development. These initiatives often involve capacity-building activities, such as training in sustainable harvesting techniques, forest monitoring, and value-added processing, which enhance community resilience and self-sufficiency.

In addition to their role in resource provision, forests offer invaluable ecosystem services that support human well-being and biodiversity. These services include water regulation, soil stabilization, and habitat provision for countless species. Forests act as natural water filters, regulating water flow and quality by absorbing rainfall and reducing runoff. This function is particularly important in regions prone to flooding or water scarcity, where forests help maintain a stable water supply. The conservation of forests, therefore, not only safeguards renewable resources but also ensures the continued provision of these life-sustaining ecosystem services.

Biodiversity conservation is another integral aspect of forestry and renewable resource management. Forests are home to an estimated 80% of terrestrial species, making them critical reservoirs of biodiversity. Sustainable forestry practices prioritize the protection of habitats and species, ensuring that the extraction of resources does not compromise ecological integrity. Conservation strategies, such as establishing protected areas and wildlife corridors, help maintain ecological connectivity and resilience, supporting the long-term survival of diverse species and ecosystems.

The integration of technology and innovation in forestry practices offers new opportunities for enhancing sustainability and efficiency. Remote sensing and geographic information systems (GIS) provide valuable data for monitoring forest conditions, assessing resource availability, and planning management activities. These tools enable forest managers to make informed decisions, optimize resource use, and minimize environmental impacts. Additionally, advances in forest certification, such as the Forest Stewardship Council (FSC) certification, provide assurance that forest products are sourced from sustainably managed forests, promoting responsible consumption and production.

Education and awareness-raising are vital components of fostering a culture of sustainability in forestry and renewable resource management. By increasing public understanding of the importance of forests and the benefits of sustainable practices, education initiatives encourage responsible behavior and support for conservation efforts. Environmental education programs, workshops, and community outreach activities engage diverse audiences, from students to policymakers, in discussions about the value of forests and the need for sustainable management.

Forestry and the management of renewable resources present both challenges and opportunities for achieving a sustainable future. The complexities of balancing resource use with conservation require a multifaceted approach that integrates science, community engagement, and policy. By embracing sustainable forestry practices, we can harness the potential of forests to provide essential resources, mitigate climate change, and support biodiversity. This commitment to stewardship invites us to reimagine our relationship with forests, recognizing their intrinsic value and their vital role in sustaining life on Earth. As we navigate the path toward sustainability, the lessons of forestry offer guidance and inspiration for nurturing a more resilient and harmonious world.

The Importance of Plant-Based Industries

Plant-based industries have emerged as powerful drivers of innovation and sustainability in the global economy. They encompass a vast array of sectors, from agriculture and textiles to pharmaceuticals and cosmetics, each harnessing the potential of plants to create products and services that meet human needs while promoting environmental stewardship. The importance of these industries lies not only in their economic contributions but also in their capacity to address pressing global challenges such as climate change, resource scarcity, and public health.

The agricultural sector forms the backbone of plant-based industries, providing essential food and raw materials for countless products. As the global population continues to rise, the demand for sustainable food production intensifies. Innovations in plant-based agriculture, such as precision farming and vertical agriculture, have revolutionized traditional farming methods, increasing efficiency and reducing environmental impact. By optimizing resource use and minimizing waste, these practices contribute to a more sustainable food system capable of feeding billions while preserving natural ecosystems.

The textile industry is another significant beneficiary of plant-based resources, with natural fibers such as cotton, linen, and hemp playing a central role in clothing and fabric production. These fibers offer renewable alternatives to synthetic materials derived from fossil fuels, reducing the industry's ecological footprint. Furthermore, the cultivation of natural fibers often requires fewer chemical inputs and less energy, contributing to lower greenhouse gas emissions. As consumers become increasingly conscious of the environmental impact of their purchasing decisions, the demand for sustainable, plant-based textiles continues to grow, driving innovation and change within the industry.

In the realm of pharmaceuticals, plant-based industries have long been a source of medicinal compounds and treatments. From the ancient use of herbs in traditional medicine to modern pharmacology, plants have provided the foundation for countless remedies and therapies. The search for new plant-derived compounds continues to fuel research and development, with many pharmaceutical companies investing in bioprospecting efforts to discover novel compounds with therapeutic potential. This exploration not only expands the arsenal of treatments available for various ailments but also underscores the critical importance of biodiversity conservation, as many medicinal plants face threats from habitat loss and overexploitation.

The cosmetics industry, too, has embraced the potential of plant-based ingredients, capitalizing on the growing consumer preference for natural and sustainable products. Plant extracts, oils, and essences are increasingly used in skincare, haircare, and personal care products, offering benefits such as hydration, nourishment, and protection. These ingredients, often sourced from sustainably managed farms, align with the industry's shift toward environmentally friendly practices and transparency in sourcing. By prioritizing plant-based formulations, cosmetic companies not only cater to consumer demands but also contribute to the preservation of ecosystems and the well-being of communities involved in raw material production.

Plant-based industries also play a pivotal role in the development of renewable energy sources. Biofuels, derived from plant materials such as corn, sugarcane, and algae, offer a renewable alternative to fossil fuels, reducing greenhouse gas emissions and dependence on non-renewable resources. The production of bioenergy, including biodiesel and bioethanol, exemplifies the potential of plants to contribute to a diversified and sustainable energy portfolio. By harnessing the energy stored in plants, these industries support efforts to transition to cleaner energy sources and mitigate the impacts of climate change.

The rise of plant-based industries is also evident in the burgeoning market for plant-based foods, such as meat and dairy alternatives. Driven by concerns over health, animal welfare, and environmental impact, consumers are increasingly seeking plant-based options that offer the taste and texture of traditional products without the associated drawbacks. This shift has spurred innovation in food technology, leading to the development of products like plant-based burgers, milk, and cheese. As these alternatives gain popularity, they contribute to a reduction in the environmental footprint of food production, as plant-based diets generally require fewer resources and produce fewer emissions than animal-based ones.

Education and advocacy are crucial in promoting the importance of plant-based industries and encouraging their growth. By raising awareness of the benefits of plant-based products and practices, educational initiatives empower consumers to make informed choices that support sustainability. Industry stakeholders, including businesses, policymakers, and researchers, play a vital role in advancing plant-based industries through collaboration, innovation, and investment in research and development. By fostering a supportive environment for plant-based industries, these efforts contribute to a more resilient and sustainable global economy.

The importance of plant-based industries extends beyond their economic contributions, as they offer solutions to some of the most pressing challenges of our time. By prioritizing sustainability, innovation, and the responsible use of natural resources, these industries pave the way for a more harmonious relationship between humanity and the planet. As we continue to explore and expand the potential of plant-based industries, we embrace a future where economic growth aligns with ecological integrity and social well-being, ensuring that the benefits of progress are shared by all. Through this commitment to sustainability and innovation, plant-based industries inspire a new era of responsible consumption and production, guiding us toward a more sustainable and equitable world.

Innovations in Plant Biotechnology

Innovations in plant biotechnology have transformed the landscape of agriculture, medicine, and environmental management over the past few decades. By harnessing the power of genetic engineering, tissue culture, and molecular biology, scientists and researchers have developed groundbreaking techniques that enhance crop productivity, improve nutritional quality, and address ecological challenges. These advancements have not only revolutionized the way we interact with plants but have also paved the way for sustainable solutions to global issues such as food security, climate change, and biodiversity conservation.

At the heart of plant biotechnology lies the manipulation of genetic material to improve plant traits. Genetic engineering, a key tool in this field, involves the insertion, deletion, or modification of specific genes within a plant's genome. This process allows for the development of genetically modified organisms (GMOs) with desirable characteristics, such as increased resistance to pests and diseases, enhanced tolerance to environmental stresses, and improved nutritional content. For example, Bt cotton, a genetically modified crop that produces a protein toxic to certain insect pests, has significantly reduced the need for chemical pesticides, leading to higher yields and lower environmental impact.

Another remarkable innovation in plant biotechnology is the development of biofortified crops, which are engineered to contain higher levels of essential nutrients. Golden Rice, a variety of rice enriched with beta-carotene, addresses vitamin A deficiency in regions where rice is a staple food. This biofortification strategy has the potential to combat malnutrition and improve public health outcomes, particularly in developing countries. By enhancing the nutritional profile of staple crops, biofortification contributes to a more balanced diet and reduces the prevalence of micronutrient deficiencies.

Tissue culture, a technique that involves the cultivation of plant cells, tissues, or organs in a controlled environment, has revolutionized plant propagation and conservation. This method allows for the rapid multiplication of plants with desirable traits, ensuring a consistent supply of high-quality planting material. Tissue culture is particularly valuable for the propagation of rare or endangered species, as it enables the production of large numbers of plants without depleting natural populations. Additionally, this technique is used in the production of disease-free planting material, which is crucial for maintaining healthy crops and improving agricultural productivity.

The advent of CRISPR-Cas9 technology has further expanded the possibilities of plant biotechnology by providing a precise and efficient tool for genome editing. This revolutionary technique allows researchers to make specific changes to a plant's DNA, enabling the development of crops with enhanced traits. CRISPR-Cas9 has been used to create disease-resistant wheat, drought-tolerant rice, and high-yielding tomatoes, among other innovations. The precision and versatility of this technology hold immense promise for addressing global challenges in agriculture and beyond.

In addition to improving crop traits, plant biotechnology plays a crucial role in environmental management and conservation. Phytoremediation, a process that uses plants to clean up contaminated soils and water, is an example of how biotechnology can address environmental pollution. Certain plants, known as hyperaccumulators, have the ability to absorb and concentrate heavy metals and other pollutants from the environment. By engineering plants with enhanced phytoremediation capabilities, scientists can develop effective strategies for restoring contaminated sites and protecting ecosystems.

Biotechnology also contributes to biodiversity conservation by facilitating the development of conservation strategies for threatened species. Molecular markers, tools used to identify specific genetic sequences, enable researchers to assess genetic diversity within and between plant populations. This information is critical for developing conservation plans that preserve genetic resources and maintain the resilience of ecosystems. By understanding the genetic makeup of plant species, conservationists can make informed decisions about habitat preservation, restoration, and management.

The integration of biotechnology into agriculture and environmental management raises important ethical and regulatory considerations. The development and use of genetically modified crops, for instance, have sparked debates about their safety, environmental impact, and socioeconomic implications. Regulatory frameworks vary across countries, with some adopting stringent measures to evaluate the risks and benefits of GMOs, while others embrace a more open approach. It is essential for policymakers, scientists, and stakeholders to engage in transparent and informed discussions to address these concerns and ensure the responsible use of biotechnological innovations.

Public perception and acceptance of plant biotechnology also play a critical role in its development and implementation. Education and outreach efforts are vital in promoting understanding of the science behind biotechnology and its potential benefits and risks. By fostering informed dialogue and addressing misconceptions, these efforts can build public trust and support for biotechnological advancements.

The future of plant biotechnology holds immense potential for addressing global challenges and improving human well-being. As research continues to advance, new innovations are likely to emerge, offering novel solutions to complex problems. Collaborative efforts between scientists, policymakers, industry, and communities will be essential in harnessing the full potential of plant biotechnology and ensuring its contributions to a sustainable and prosperous future.

The journey of plant biotechnology is one of innovation, exploration, and transformation. By unlocking the potential of plants at the molecular level, this field offers powerful tools for enhancing agricultural productivity, conserving biodiversity, and restoring ecosystems. As we continue to push the boundaries of what is possible, plant biotechnology inspires a vision of a future where human ingenuity and nature work in harmony to create a better world. Through responsible stewardship and collaboration, we can harness the potential of plant biotechnology to address the challenges of today and build a foundation for a sustainable tomorrow.

The Future of Sustainable Plant Economies

Sustainable plant economies are rapidly emerging as vital components of the global strategy to tackle pressing environmental and economic challenges. The future of these economies promises a harmonious integration of ecological balance and economic growth, achieved through innovative practices and technologies. By focusing on the sustainable management of plant resources, we can unlock pathways to a more resilient and equitable world.

At the core of sustainable plant economies is the principle of using resources in a manner that meets current needs without compromising future generations. This involves adopting practices that enhance biodiversity, improve soil health, and reduce carbon footprints. In agriculture, for instance, the shift towards regenerative farming techniques reflects this commitment. By employing crop rotation, cover cropping, and reduced tillage, regenerative agriculture enhances soil fertility, sequesters carbon, and promotes biodiversity. These practices not only increase agricultural productivity but also contribute to climate resilience and ecosystem restoration.

Urban agriculture is gaining traction as cities look for ways to become more self-sufficient and reduce their environmental impact. By integrating food production into urban landscapes through rooftop gardens, vertical farms, and community plots, cities can address food security, reduce transportation emissions, and create green spaces. Urban agriculture also fosters community involvement and education, enhancing social cohesion and awareness of sustainable practices.

The textile industry is another area where plant-based solutions are driving sustainability. Natural fibers, such as organic cotton and hemp, are being embraced as alternatives to synthetic materials. These fibers require fewer resources and have a lower environmental impact, aligning with the goals of a circular economy. Additionally, innovations in textile recycling and upcycling are reducing waste and extending the life cycle of garments, contributing to a more sustainable fashion industry.

In the energy sector, plant-based innovations are playing a critical role in the transition to renewable energy sources. Biofuels derived from plant materials like algae and crop residues offer a sustainable alternative to fossil fuels, reducing greenhouse gas emissions and dependence on non-renewable resources. The development of bioplastics, made from renewable plant sources, is also gaining momentum. These materials provide an eco-friendly alternative to conventional plastics, reducing pollution and the environmental impact of plastic production and disposal.

Pharmaceutical and cosmetic industries are increasingly turning to plants for sustainable solutions. Plant-based compounds continue to be explored for their medicinal and therapeutic properties, offering new treatments and improving health outcomes. In cosmetics, the demand for natural, plant-derived ingredients is on the rise, driven by consumer preferences for transparency and environmental responsibility.

Education plays a crucial role in advancing sustainable plant economies. By raising awareness of the benefits and potential of sustainable practices, educational programs empower individuals and communities to make informed decisions. Initiatives such as workshops, community events, and school curricula promote understanding and engagement, fostering a culture of sustainability that supports the growth of plant-based industries.

Policy development is another critical factor in the success of sustainable plant economies. Governments and regulatory bodies are increasingly recognizing the need for frameworks that support sustainable practices and innovation. By providing incentives for research and development, implementing standards for sustainable production, and facilitating collaboration among stakeholders, policymakers can create an enabling environment for sustainable plant economies to thrive.

The journey towards sustainable plant economies presents both challenges and opportunities. It requires a rethinking of conventional practices and a commitment to innovation and collaboration. By leveraging the potential of plants and integrating ecological principles into economic systems, we can create resilient economies that benefit both people and the planet.

The potential of sustainable plant economies is vast and transformative. By embracing these principles and practices, we can address complex global challenges while fostering economic growth and social equity. The future of sustainable plant economies is one of hope and progress, offering a vision of a world where human prosperity and environmental health go hand in hand. Through collaboration and innovation, we can build a future where sustainable plant economies flourish, supporting a thriving and resilient world for generations to come.